Australian Biographical Monographs

20

Australian Biographical Monographs

Series Editor: Scott Prasser

Previous Volumes

Joseph Cook	Zachary Gorman
Annabelle Rankin	Peter Sekuless
Robert (Bob) Hawke	Mike Steketee
John Curtin	David Lee
Jack Lang	David Clune
Leonie Kramer	Damien Freeman
Margaret Guilfoyle	Anne Henderson
William McKell	David Clune
Neville Bonner	Sean Jacobs
George Reid	Luke Walker
Robert Askin	Paul Loughnan
John Grey Gorton	Paul Williams
Stanley Melbourne Bruce	David Lee
Robert Menzies	Scott Prasser
Neville Wran	David Clune
Lindsay Thompson	William Westerman
Johannes Bjelke-Petersen	Bruce Kingston
Harold Holt	Tom Frame
Joseph Lyons	Kevin Andrews

Australian Biographical Monographs

20

Arthur Calwell

TRANSFORMING AUSTRALIA THROUGH IMMIGRATION

James Franklin

Gerry O Nolan

Connor Court Publishing

Australian Biographical Monographs 20
Arthur Calwell by James Franklin and Gerry O Nolan

Published in 2023 by Connor Court Publishing Pty Ltd

Copyright © James Franklin and Gerry O Nolan

All rights reserved. No part of this book may be reproduced or transmitted in any form or by any means, electronic or mechanical, including photo copying, recording or by any information storage and retrieval system, without prior permission in writing from the publisher.

Connor Court Publishing Pty Ltd
PO Box 7257
Redland Bay QLD 4165
sales@connorcourt.com
www.connorcourt.com

Printed in Australia

ISBN: 978-1-922815-81-1

Front Cover Photograph: Cover image, Portrait of Arthur A. Calwell, 1945 [picture] / Max Dupain: https://nla.gov.au/nla.obj-137140311/view

The days of our isolation are over. We live in an age when the earth's surface seems to be contracting under the influence of scientific discoveries...The call to all Australians is to realise that without adequate numbers this wide brown land may not be held in another clash of arms..."

Calwell CPD, HR, 11 November 1946 vol 189, p. 511.

Series overview

Connor Court's *Australian Biographical Series* on past leading Australian political leaders and other important figures seeks to provide an overview for those who are unfamiliar with the subject and to highlight the person's particular importance, controversies, and contributions to Australia's progress.

The monographs are scholarly rather than academic in focus, placing emphasis on a clear narrative, but with careful attention to referencing to ensure views expressed are supported by appropriate sources and evidence.

The Series was initiated because of the decline in the study of Australian history at our schools and universities. Consequently, there has been a lack of knowledge or, even worse, distorted views, of some of Australia's leading historical figures who deserve to be remembered, better understood for their achievements, and, as each volume also highlights, their flaws.

It has been nearly fifty years since there has been a biography of Arthur Calwell, Labor federal member from 1940-1972, Minister for Immigration and later leader of the Opposition. His massive immigration program in the immediate postwar period began the transformation of Australia to a multicultural nation. Calwell served under the best (Chifley) and possibly the most difficult (Evatt) of the Labor leaders, remained loyal to the Labor cause when it split in the mid 1950s when its future looked bleak. Yet, after becoming leader in 1960 he almost defeated then Prime Minister Menzies at the 1961 election and did much to restore Labor's faith in itself as well as to renew policy for the nation. However, two subsequent election defeats in 1963 and 1966 meant Calwell had to make way for the younger Gough Whitlam in 1967. He retired at the 1972 election which saw Labor finally back in office. So, this is a story of conviction, belief and for Labor federal members, during the long period of 23 years in the political wilderness, of immense resilience – personally as well as politically.

This new monograph, researched by Professor James Franklin with Gerry O Nolan not only refreshes our memory about Arthur Calwell, the long serving politician, but also Calwell the man, including his Catholic religious beliefs which figured far more prominently in public life and personal considerations than for most politicians today.

James Franklin's previous books on Australian history are *Corrupting the Youth: A History of Philosophy in Australia*, *The Real Archbishop Mannix*, with Gerry O Nolan, *and Catholic Thought and Catholic Action: Scenes from Australian Catholic Life.* He is Honorary Professor at the University of New South Wales, Sydney and editor of the *Journal of the Australian Catholic Historical Society.*

■ Scott Prasser

Introduction

On 7 December 1947, Arthur Calwell, Australia's first Minister for Immigration, stood at the dockside in Port Melbourne to meet *HMAS Kanimbla*. The ship brought some 850 refugees from the Baltic states. They were the first shipment of over 170,000 Displaced Persons, Eastern European refugees from the Red Army who had been languishing in camps for years. These "New Australians", as Calwell termed them, were followed by millions of other non-English-speakers in the decades ahead, transforming Australia from "a dull inbred country of predominantly British stock" (Calwell's words)[1] to the dynamic multicultural nation of today.

The arrival of the *Kanimbla* was the culmination of an extraordinary planning effort after a period of extreme frustration, during which Calwell's many efforts to find immigrants to satisfy Australia's new "Populate or perish" policy had come to nothing. He signed an agreement only on 21 July 1947 with the International Refugee Organisation (IRO). The first refugees were selected very quickly by Australian agents in Germany and were got through the ravaged German transport system for embarkation at Bremerhaven on 30 October. They were hand-picked to head off a feared xenophobic reaction in Australia, which was unused to significant numbers of non-English-speaking immigrants. As Calwell later wrote in his autobiography,

> We would bring one shipload with nobody under fifteen and nobody over thirty-five, all of whom had to be single. ... Many were red-headed and blue-eyed. There was also a number of natural platinum blondes of both sexes. The men were handsome and the women beautiful. It was not hard to sell immigration to the Australian people once the press published photographs of that group.[2]

Photographed next to Calwell, they looked better still. The publicity campaign was an unqualified success, paving the way for huge numbers of Eastern and Southern European and later Asian immigrants.

Arthur Calwell's reputation has suffered from being seen from the future looking back. Most recollections of him as a public figure date from the 1960s, when he was an aged and unsuccessful leader of the Federal opposition. Just failing to win the 1961 election despite gaining some 50.5% of the two-party-preferred vote, his chances waned as he vainly fought the popularity of the Menzies-Holt government and its Vietnam commitment and defended the outmoded White Australia Policy. The 1950s were a difficult time for him too, when he was a loyal deputy Labor leader to the barely sane Dr Evatt and embroiled in the agonies of the Labor Split of 1954–5. Memories of those hard times have overshadowed his achievements of the 1940s and his leading role in the Curtin and Chifley governments, especially as Minister for Immigration.

Growing up before World War I in crowded inner-city Melbourne, with its cramped cottages built on sixteen-feet frontages, the young Calwell was surrounded by poverty and misery, and, like many others, committed himself to Labor politics to relieve it – and often to the more socialist of Labor policies, though he was always staunchly anti-Communist. In a political career of over fifty years, he never wavered in support for the party and in unrelenting work on its behalf. As he expressed clearly in his 1963 manifesto, *Labor's Role in Modern Society*, he was supremely confident that he knew what was good for the average Australian, he knew where he was going and where he wanted himself and the Labor Party to go.

He was equally committed to his Catholic faith – indeed, he was the most flamboyantly Catholic of all major Australian political leaders. Archbishop Mannix was both hero and mentor, for the fifty years from the day Calwell saw the new coadjutor Archbishop arrive at Spencer Street Station, to the day he wept at his deathbed – despite serious differences during the Split of the 1950s. He was created a papal knight in 1964 for his services to immigration.

Support for Ireland was another early enthusiasm, and like his other interests, pursued with great thoroughness. Calwell learned Irish Gaelic and addressed part of the great Richmond Racecourse meeting of 1917 in Gaelic. In 1918 he was arrested and interrogated by security forces for his role in the Young Ireland Society, which was suspected of sympathy with Sinn Fein. His admiration for Ireland implied a lower degree of enthusiasm than most Australians felt for the British Empire and the domination of Australian public life by Protestants of British ancestry and conservative opinions. The immigration program gave him the opportunity to make changes to that – in the longer term, massive changes.

A rather lanky, bespectacled and beak-nosed man, with a thatch of hair in which there was a glint of red, Calwell had an extraordinarily precise vocabulary and the gift for a telling and often cutting phrase. The language was backed by strong emotion. While some saw him as a great hater, according to his own account:

> I've always been a rather a volatile character in Australian politics. I blame all that on to my grandmothers. When the Welsh blood cooled down, the Irish blood warmed up and so I was never out of strife. But I have no regrets. I fought the good fight according to my own views, and I took some pretty heavy defeats. I have no regrets about those defeats, and I have no bitterness to anybody.[3]

The times after 1950 were unkind to him and he saw little but defeats, some the fault of others and some not. But Australia at the time of his death and later was a very different country from the one it would have been without his success with immigration in the 1940s.

1

Personal

Born on 28 August 1896 in West Melbourne, Arthur Calwell was the eldest of seven children brought up in a hardscrabble inner-city Irish-Catholic working class area.[4] Later in his life he noted, "I grew up in [the] crowded inner [city] area, with evidence of human misery visible to all." When six years of age, he suffered a near fatal attack of diphtheria, to which he attributed the "high-pitched huskiness" of his voice.

Calwell was raised in the Catholic faith of his Irish maternal grandmother, and his mother, who died when he was 16 at the age of 40, leaving seven children. His father, an Anglican, was a policeman, later in a senior role. His paternal great-grandfather had served briefly in the Pennsylvania legislature in the 1820s. He attended St Joseph's Christian Brothers' College, North Melbourne and on 28 March 1913, upon matriculation, entered the Victorian Public Service as a clerk in the Department of Agriculture, later moving to the Treasury. During World War I he twice applied for an army commission but was rejected.

He was a man of ideas as well as action and continued his political education by reading, mainly in the left-wing classics such as the English Chartists, the British Labour leader Keir Hardie, the Fabians, Edward Bellamy, Robert Owen, Dickens and Savonarola. Catholic reading included such titles as *A Course of Instruction for Catholic*

Youth, Meditations for Lay Folk and lives of Augustine, Joan of Arc and Therese of Lisieux and writings of John Henry Newman.[5]

He defied public service regulations against open involvement in politics and, while still in his teens, became secretary of the Melbourne branch of the Australian Labor Party. He served loyally in local Labor politics for decades until elected Federal member for Melbourne in 1940.

In 1921, he married Margaret Murphy, who died just five months later. In 1932, he married Elizabeth Marren, an Irishwoman who was social editor of the weekly Catholic newspaper *The Tribune*. Calwell met Elizabeth through Irish language classes run by the Gaelic League in Melbourne, where he learned Gaelic and retained an interest in and fluency in it. In 1933 they launched the *Irish Review* as the official organ of the Victorian Irish Association. Its stories of Ireland and its culture were strongly positive.

Elizabeth and Arthur had two children, Mary Elizabeth and Arthur Andrew. Arthur Andrew died of leukemia aged eleven in 1948, at the time of his father's success as Minister for Immigration. His father was devastated, the blow striking him "with all the force of a bombshell". From the day his son died until his own death, Calwell wore a black neck-tie in his son's remembrance. Mrs Elizabeth Calwell later recalled: "That was the cruellest blow Arthur has ever suffered. In fact he has never been the same since that dreadful day."[6]

The early deaths of his mother, first wife and son, with the thwarting of his prime ministerial ambitions in 1961, were a higher quota of tragedy than most people experience.

He was always very careful of what clothes he wore. Almost invariably, he wore a lounge suit, white shirt and black tie. He never drove a motor car, relying always on public transport or on the Commonwealth car available to him.

He never smoked and he drank alcoholic beverages in moderation, chiefly whisky. He read widely and had a good knowledge of Australian and Irish history. He bought many books, had a large library and liked to discuss historical topics.

Calwell was devoted to his wife and family and took all of his responsibilities very seriously. When he chose to be, he was a good listener, particularly if his interlocutor was troubled. He possessed two personal qualities very useful for a politician, an enormous capacity for hard work and a prodigious memory for both facts and people – many were surprised when he remembered them years after a brief meeting.[7] Although known for his feuds, he had the ability to get on well at a personal level with some on the other side of politics, such as Menzies, of whom he always spoke with politeness and respect.

2

Political apprenticeship in Labor and Irish politics (1896–1939)

In 1914, at about the same time he joined the Labor Party, Calwell joined the Young Ireland Society. In the heated patriotic atmosphere of the War, Irish sympathies became suddenly suspect after the Easter Rising of 1916, when a small group of Irish republicans staged an unexpected and short-lived rebellion in Dublin. Led by Archbishop Mannix, Australian sympathisers with Ireland voted against the Conscription Referendums of 1916 and 1917, leading to widespread perceptions of disloyalty and of shirking the war effort.

Calwell had a small role in the largest anti-conscription meeting, held at Richmond Racecourse in November 1917. The Young Ireland Society hired the Melbourne Exhibition Building for a rally to be held on the eve of the Melbourne Cup. However, a deputation representing the Loyal Orange Institution and the Protestant Alliance Friendly Society called on the premier to tell him that, "Protestants were apprehensive that the peace of the community would be seriously disturbed." The trustees backed down and cancelled the meeting. (Mannix said "not fit to be trustees of a Punch and Judy show ... as much backbone as a stick of boiled asparagus", in a style of rhetoric from which Calwell learned something.)

The Young Ireland Society with Mannix reconvened at Richmond racecourse where Mannix addressed an estimated 100,000 people. Mannix said that Australians without knowing it were really Sinn Feiners, and continued, "Now my advice, if I could give it to the Irish people ... I can at all events whisper it to you ... don't wait until England's plight with the war is over, it is NOW or NEVER for Home Rule."[8] In the days before loudspeakers could reach a huge audience, portions of the crowd were addressed by other speakers. Calwell, speaking in Gaelic, was one of them.[9]

His activities as secretary of the Young Ireland Society brought him under the surveillance of security authorities. Having become secretary of a Labor Party branch, Calwell received a considerable amount of literature from various union and socialist groups as well as some pamphlets about the Irish troubles. In 1918, at the age of 22, he was picked up and interviewed by security as a possible Sinn Fein activist. He reports on the incident:

> I knew that I was being reported on and, eventually I found myself confronted by two Victorian detectives ...
>
> They told my father, who was then a senior constable of police, about my activities. Then they picked me up at a CMF refresher course in 1918 and took me home, where they examined all the literature I had in my possession. All the literature had come to me by virtue of my secretaryship of the Melbourne branch of the Australian Labor Party, a position which I took over at the age of eighteen. There were letters which I had received from the Industrial Workers of the World, there were letters from various socialist groups, and there was a pile

> of anti-conscription letters and literature and some pamphlets about the Irish troubles. The detectives took all these documents away with them, and I had to attend the Victoria Barracks next day. I was questioned there for an hour and a half, but nothing further happened.[10]

The security forces were right in their conclusion that he was not a danger to security.

While Mannix vigorously promoted Irish republicanism and was arrested on the high seas by the Royal Navy in 1920 to prevent his stepping foot in Ireland, most Australian Irish sympathisers, Calwell among them, lost interest in Irish politics by the time of the Irish Civil War (1922–3). Calwell did, however, unusually pursue Irish cultural interests. And he never lost an Irish sense that the Protestant ascendancy was not the natural or inevitable order of things.

While the Labor Party's opposition to conscription had deepened Calwell's appreciation of the Party, it was his own energy and ability that ensured his progress within the movement. Calwell had begun his public career in the Victorian Public Service in 1913 as a clerk in the Department of Agriculture. He was elected to the state executive in the same year, and was state president of the party from 1930 to 1931 – at the time, the youngest person to have held the position. He served as foundation president of the Clerical Division of the Australian Public Service Association (Victorian Branch) 1925–31. Other positions from the 1930s include President of North Melbourne Football Club, trustee of the Melbourne Cricket Ground and Alderman of Melbourne City Council. He was becoming central to how

Melbourne worked.

In 1935, in what was to be the first of many clashes with the press, he gained £150 and an apology from the *Herald* for an article that implied a conflict between his public service role and Labor political activities.[11]

Throughout the 1930s he marshalled Victorian Labor against the rebel New South Wales Labor Party and its fiery leader Jack Lang. Calwell's collaboration with the federal parliamentary leader John Curtin culminated in the unity conference of August 1939 which broke Lang's power in New South Wales.

After the Depression he devoted an increasing amount of his time to the electoral affairs of the Federal constituency of Melbourne, a safe Labor seat. The seat had been held since 1904 by William Maloney; indeed, Calwell's first political memory was of being taken as an eight-year-old to hear his speech in that campaign.[12] Dr Maloney had been a labour member of the Victorian Parliament in the 1880s, before the Labor Party existed, and was aged 80 in 1934. Nevertheless Calwell remained loyal to him and made no attempt to persuade the "Little Doctor" to stand aside or to seek preselection elsewhere.

Maloney died in August 1940. Prime Minister Menzies had called a federal election for 21 September 1940 and the Victorian Executive as expected endorsed Calwell for Melbourne. Calwell won the seat and held it easily until his retirement.

In summary, Arthur Calwell was a member of the Australian Labor Party from 1914 until 1973; president of the Victorian branch 1930–31, Member of the House of Representatives for Melbourne, 1940–72; Minister for Information 1943–49; Minister for Immigration 1945–49; Deputy Leader of the Opposition 1951–60; Leader of the Opposition from 7 March 1960; until 8 February 1967, when he was succeeded by Gough Whitlam.

3

Election to Parliament and Minister for Information (1940-44)

Arthur Calwell's maiden speech, when he was finally elected to Federal Parliament in 1940, reveals the issues that were close to his heart. Appropriately for a future Minister for Immigration, his main concern was population. A rapidly declining birthrate after 1900, and especially during the Depression, had been a concern of many Western countries, but it was a special issue for Australia with its population of only seven million in a vast continent. The threat from populous nations to the north had not yet materialised, but the fall of Singapore to the Japanese was not much more than a year in the future. His solution was at this stage not immigration but support for births, especially child endowment and baby health centres.

Some substantial extracts from his speech show Calwell's passionate commitment to the cause of population as well as his forceful mode of expression. After calling attention to official predictions that the Australian population will decline from 1955, he continues:

> Although we are but 150 years old as a nation, apparently we are slowly bleeding to death, and within a 200 year period this outpost of white civilization in the Pacific will have almost entirely disappeared. Yet this Government, which is acquainted with the facts, neither does nor suggests

anything, but resists every attempt that we make on humanitarian and national grounds to establish a scheme of child endowment or family allowance, because under such a scheme those of their friends who benefited from the work of the community would have to pay.

The Government is neither courageous nor wise enough to take time by the forelock and do what should be done. It would appear that only one honorable gentleman opposite has interested himself in this problem; he is the septuagenarian Minister for the Navy (Mr. Hughes). He is the only one who has told this country that it must either populate or perish.

(The slogan "populate or perish", though not Calwell's invention, came to be strongly associated with him in the years ahead.)

The Nazis, he points out, have been doing a better job:

> One of the chief preoccupations of National-Socialist Germany was population. The decline of the German birth rate from the beginning of this century until 1933 had been catastrophic. Professor Lodewyckx made the following observations on the subject: However, soon after the National Socialist Party took office early in 1933, energetic measures were adopted in an endeavour to stop the downward trend. These measures may be summed up under the following four headings:
>
> 1. Direct financial advantages to large families and

to newly-married couples.

2. Reduction of unemployment.

3. Intensive propaganda aiming at a new outlook on population problems amongst the whole people.

4. Stricter enforcement of the law prohibiting the practice of abortion.

The result has been a substantial increase in the birth-rate. The numbers of births registered for the years 1933 to 1937 are as follows: 1933, 971,000 births; 1934, 1,198,000 births; 1935, 1,264,000 births, 1936, 1,297,000 births; 1937, 1,276,000 births.

The record of Australia in relation to the birth-rate is such as to demand serious consideration. Our birth-rate fell from 4.3 per 1,000 of the population in 1862 to 1.7 per 1,000 in 1937. The effect can be expressed in another way: In 1911, when Australia had a population of roughly 4,500,000, more children were born than in 1938, when our population was approaching 7,000,000. This problem cannot be ignored, and we cannot procrastinate in dealing with it if we wish to continue to progress as a white nation.[13]

Other policies he advocated were public health centres and kindergartens – for which he praised Melbourne City Council – and marriage loans. The age of marriage had risen considerably during the Depression as couples postponed marriage for financial reasons.

Child endowment was instituted in 1941 (at 5 shillings per

week for children other than the first), but by the Menzies Government. It proved a popular and successful policy. Its role in the postwar "Baby Boom" is hard to evaluate.

The Fadden Government, which briefly succeeded the Menzies Government, fell in late 1941 and John Curtin became Prime Minister. He soon had to face the outbreak of war in the Pacific and, with the fall of Singapore and Japanese penetration almost to Australia, the greatest threat Australia has ever faced to its existence. Calwell was a senior Labor figure and active in Caucus, but too new as a member of parliament for ministerial office. Despite the crisis, his actions were not those of a "team player" and he clashed personally with Curtin many times. He described frankly their bad relations:

> [Curtin] held a slumbering resentment against me. I might have invited some of his resentment because of my refusal to compromise or meet his wishes ...

> Another time, Curtin came to me and said, 'Come around and have a cup of tea.' I replied, 'No thanks.' I resented the treatment I had received. For some time after that, Curtin became even more hostile towards me. He ignored me and spurned me. One day when I was mounting the steps near his office in Parliament House, he saw me and immediately went back to his room. There were other times he would not speak to me ... and I, therefore, would not speak to him.[14]

The issue on which they clashed most fiercely was conscription. Although Curtin had been a strong anti-conscriptionist in the First War, he decided the gravity of the war situation required conscription, with conscripts deployed only to territories near Australia. Calwell was the leading Labor opponent of the policy. Conflict also arose over the balance between the war effort and domestic policy. Calwell reports:

> My worst experience with Curtin occurred at a meeting of the Federal Labor Party on March 24, 1943. I had been pressing hard for social changes even in the midst of war, in line with our socialist policy. Curtin believed we should win the war first, and leave most matters concerning the post-war situation to be gradually developed as time went on.
>
> Curtin was in the chair and he said to me in the most sneering way, 'The hero of 100 sham fights!'
>
> I retorted at once, 'It's all very well for you to say that, but the way you're going you'll finish up on the other side, leading a National Government.'
>
> Curtin rose immediately and left the room. Pandemonium broke out. I realized immediately that I should not have replied to his bitter taunt in the way I did. I said to Frank Forde, who had taken Curtin's place in the chair: 'Mr Chairman, I withdraw that remark and I apologize.'[15]

After the election of 1943, which Labor won convincingly, Calwell was elevated to Cabinet as Minister for Information. "Information" was largely a euphemism for censorship and propaganda. They were difficult issues in wartime with the need to maintain morale by, for example, suppressing information about the chaos following the bombing of Darwin in early 1942. Calwell took an aggressive attitude to press complaints about censorship, fuelled by traditional Labor hatred of conservative "press barons" – he had said in parliament in 1941 that the press "is owned for the most part by financial crooks and is edited for the most part by mental harlots. These are the people who at election time misrepresent the principles and policy of the Labor Party, and theirs are the newspapers which libel, malign, traduce, and defame us."[16]

During the temporary absence of Curtin, a former journalist, in 1944, the proprietors of the four Sydney morning papers formed an alliance to take Calwell on and employed expensive lawyers. Comparisons of Calwell with Goebbels were sent in to provoke the censors.

Matters came to a head when the *Sunday Telegraph* of 16 April 1944 printed blank space on part the front page to denote censorship. Above was a photograph of Calwell, alongside one of Rupert Henderson, chairman of the Australian Newspaper Proprietors' Association, whose speech criticising censorship had itself been censored. (Text cut by the censor included "Mr Calwell has abused his ministerial powers to persecute a newspaper because it has found it necessary to criticise him as a public man ... how important it is to defend our free institutions against tin-pot dictators.") Within the otherwise blank space appeared a short entry surrounded by a black line: "A free press? The great American democrat Thomas Jefferson said, 'Where the Press is free and every man able to read, all is safe.'" Commonwealth peace officers (forerunners of the Federal Police) were sent to the loading docks of the *Telegraph* and other papers to seize all undistributed copies. Some of the officers unwisely posed with revolvers, leading to perfect press photos. The metropolitan dailies took up the issue vigorously the next day and were themselves suppressed.

The newspapers then successfully sought an injunction from the High Court to prevent suppression and the government backed down.[17]

Cartoonist John Frith was given a generous increase in salary for his cartoons picturing Calwell as a cranky cockatoo on a perch shrieking "Curse the press!"

The censorship issue and Calwell's problems with the press simmered with varying degrees of heat in subsequent decades. In the 1950s he fought unsuccessfully the media empires' expansion into commercial television, which he predicted would be "like imported comics and just as educational".[18] In the elections of the 1960s adverse publicity was to play a role in denying him the prime ministership of Australia.

During the War Calwell also held the position of Chairman of the Aliens Classification and Advisory Committee, which dealt with the many Italian Australians interned early in the War as a possible security risk. The Committee decided that most of the internees were loyal Australians and could be released. It was useful experience in understanding the benefits to Australia of European immigrants.[19]

As the tide of war turned from 1943, those like Calwell who advocated more attention to social issues at home were able to make more headway. Ben Chifley as Minister for Postwar Reconstruction – and often as de facto Prime Minister when Curtin's health failed – oversaw ambitious plans to change Australia dramatically as soon as the War was over. Social security would be extended widely, large national infrastructure projects like the Snowy Mountains Scheme would be undertaken, government would intervene more forcefully in finance, international security efforts like the United Nations would be supported. And the shock of near-invasion in 1942 had convinced traditionally anti-immigration Labor leaders that, as part of the mix, massive numbers of migrants would be needed. Initial planning envisaged the possibility of southern and eastern Europeans as well as British. Calwell wrote confidentially to Chifley in 1944 of his "... determination to develop a heterogeneous society: a society where Irishness and Roman Catholicism would be as acceptable as Englishness and Protestantism; where an Italian background would be as acceptable as a Greek, a Dutch or any other."[20]

It was pure speculation, however, whether any such migrants would be available.

4

Minister for Immigration: The Search for Immigrants (1945-47)

Curtin died on 7 July 1945 and Ben Chifley was elected as Labor leader and hence Prime Minister. By then the War was in its last stages, although its sudden end with the atomic bombs was still in the near future. Bolstered by a convincing win in the election of 1946, the Chifley Government was free to pursue most of its interventionist agenda.

Calwell was appointed Minister for Immigration, the first in Australian history, with strong support from Chifley to pursue a vigorous program of bringing migrants to Australia. Support in some other quarters, such as the trade unions and the general public, was more doubtful, but the shock of near-invasion by the Japanese was only three years in the past and the slogan "populate or perish" was widely accepted.

The commitment raised many difficult questions, all of which needed answers very quickly. What types of immigrants were desirable? Where would they be found? How would they be selected? How would they be brought to Australia and would the government pay? Would the Australian people accept them? What would be done with them when they arrived?

In addition to deciding these questions in principle, a departmental structure had to be created from scratch to carry out the plans. As with any great plan, it was not a one-man show and the dedicated team who worked on it should be remembered. Calwell was fortunate to find a talented and hard-working group to implement his plans, notably departmental head Tasman Heyes ("ranks with the best and most highly successful departmental heads in the history of our Federation," in Calwell's words),[21] private secretary Bob Armstrong, Noel Lamidey who was in charge of migration at Australia House in London,[22] and, in charge of selection in the European camps, the colourful Brigadier "Black Jack" Galleghan, former commander of the Australian troops in Changi.[23] His long-term secretary (personal assistant in later terminology) Joan O'Donnell was essential to organisation at home, as was the support of his wife and daughter.

Immigrants first had to be white. Calwell was and always remained a strong supporter of the White Australia policy, for reasons to be discussed in a later chapter, and that policy had general popular support although some favoured making exceptions. Of white ethnicities, those who had fought on the wrong side in the War, such as Germans, would have to wait a while (though a few German technical experts were accepted[24]) and war criminals were excluded as far as possible. In the emerging Cold War atmosphere, being too left-wing was also problematic – at one point the French offered some refugees left over from the Spanish Civil War but the offer was declined.[25] Jews were acceptable and Calwell called for humanitarian immigration when the Holocaust was revealed in 1945, although some restrictions were placed on the numbers in any one shipload to avoid provoking anti-semitic reaction; some

20,000 came up to 1951 (on both assisted and private schemes) and Australia came to have proportionately the highest number of Holocaust survivors of any country other than Israel.[26]

That left as possible sources Britain, the traditional origin of the vast majority of immigrants to Australia since 1900; other Anglophone countries such as Ireland, the United States and Canada; and continental Europe. It was initially assumed that Britain would be the main source and it seemed very hopeful, as the disruptions of the War and subsequent austerity made many Britons think of emigrating to somewhere sunnier and richer. Indeed many did come from 1948 as shipping became available, some one million arriving between then and 1980. However, as Britain began reconstruction and the welfare state promised a better life for the poor, interest from Britons fell and it was clear that other sources would be needed. Calwell's Irish and Catholic background meant that he was somewhat less enthusiastic about Britons that the average Australian, though he was happy enough if they made up the numbers. His assurance in his first ministerial speech that there would be ten Britons for every migrant of alien origin can be taken with a grain of salt. Ireland, the United States and Canada, which had avoided the direct effects of war, proved to have very few people interested in emigration. That left Eastern and Southern Europe, in many parts devastated by the War and full of refugees eager to go anywhere else.

Australia preferred able-bodied men and women, and children who would more easily become Australians, but did not plan to break up families. Calwell was happy with intellectuals, doctors and professionals but the professional associations in Australia, especially the all-powerful British Medical Association (Australian branches) prevented the recognition of foreign qualifications.[27] Migrants were to be healthy – especially, free of TB.

Australia demanded the right to select immigrants individually. Staff at Australia House in London could deal with British applicants, but selection in European refugee camps would require staff with security skills.

The main logistic difficulty, as was clear from the beginning, was lack of shipping. A substantial portion of the British and United States merchant navies had been sunk by U-boats, and the remainder, with new ships, had more important work than transporting migrants on the long voyage to Australia – reviving trade and being ready for troop transport in the event of a likely European war against the Soviet Union. The shipping shortage was the main reason why by mid-1947, halfway through Calwell's tenure as Minister for Immigration, the immigration program remained a near-total failure, with very few migrant ships having arrived. A particularly frustrating event was the falling through at the last moment of a plan to lease a British aircraft carrier for a Catholic child migration scheme.

Nevertheless, Calwell himself believed that the main problem for his scheme was neither sourcing of migrants nor logistics but their possible rejection by the Australian people. Although the Australian states in the nineteenth century had been immigrant societies with close to free immigration, that was not the case with Australia after 1901. The White Australia Policy explicitly excluded many races, but immigration other than from Britain was also unpopular. Ben Chifley had been elected to parliament in 1928 with a viciously xenophobic campaign against "hundreds of Italians, Jugo-Slavians and Czecho-Slovakians", "scabs of the worst kind", working on the Melbourne waterfront while Australians were left to walk the streets and their wives and children starved.[28] Many other union men instinctively saw immigrants as a threat to jobs, and non-British ones as likely to accept lower wages than Australians. A mere 7000 Jewish refugees just before the Second World War had provoked considerable reaction to the strange ways of "reffos". While the federal opposition led by Menzies supported the postwar program, its acceptance by other groups, especially trade unions and the press, was far from assured. Calwell's bad relations with the press did not bode well.

A particular difficulty at the receiving end was that building had been neglected during the Depression and War and there was a gross shortage of housing and of building materials. British immigrants could perhaps be left to look after themselves after a period in hostels, provided that unemployment remained low, but it was otherwise if non-English-speaking refugees were to be admitted. They would need jobs and accommodation provided somehow. One possible kind of accommodation, for those not too demanding of standards, was now-vacant army camps.

Calwell threw himself into the task with great energy,

but for a long time with little success.

For Britons, the Assisted Passage Migration Scheme, or "Ten Pound Poms" was instituted in 1945. For ten pounds sterling (children free), a passage was provided with some later assistance in migrant hostels.[29] The British were initially keen and by 1947, after a horrendous winter made worse by strikes, some 400,000 Britons were registered at Australia House for the scheme. But with the shipping shortage, getting any substantial numbers to Australia proved near-impossible well into 1947.

Then the Cold War intervened. It came to light that a million refugees were available in Europe. As they threatened to destabilise Europe, there was enough motivation to find ships to take them elsewhere.

In the chaos of the sudden collapse of Nazism in 1945 and the ensuing "Iron Curtain" standoff between East and West, one significant problem was the millions of refugees who had fled the advance of the Red Army and were left in Western Europe. At first, many were sent home to be shot, but as the Cold War developed and the appetite for cooperating with Soviet demands waned, a million were left in camps in Germany, Austria and Italy. They mostly came from the Eastern European countries with traditional antipathies to Russia – Poland, Ukraine and the Baltic countries (Lithuania, Latvia and Estonia). Having fled the Red Army in fear of their lives, they were fiercely anti-communist. Many were able-bodied and well-educated. When the political situation stabilised in 1946, the Western powers making major decisions on Cold War policy –

principally Britain and the United States – were faced with the problem of what to do with the refugees, now called "Displaced Persons" or DPs.[30]

A comprehensive solution was sought to the problem of European refugees in camps. A United Nations sponsored anti-communist body, the International Refugee Organisation (IRO), was set up to both administer the camps and organise emigration. Jewish refugees could be sent to Palestine when part of that region was given to the new state of Israel. It was harder to find somewhere to send the rest. They could not be dispersed into the countries where the camps were located – as well as being devastated by the War and being politically unstable, they were the frontline states against the Iron Curtain and needed all the support they could get, without the additional problem of absorbing refugees of different ethnicities. In addition, Germany had to assimilate some ten million German refugees from the east. The USA was also not possible; although President Truman was eager to help, an isolationist Congress prevented large-scale immigration until 1948. Britain itself began to take considerable numbers from 1946, but its capacity was limited by its own economic problems.

Some more distant countries would have to help. South American countries took an early lead, and Canada was helpful with Poles. But British thinking naturally turned to another country which had wide open spaces, a solid economy and a long track record as a dumping ground for people surplus to British requirements. It also had a government ideologically aligned with the

Attlee Labour Government and so possibly prepared to offer some fraternal help. In March 1947, Viscount Addison, Secretary of State for Dominion Affairs, wrote to the Australian High Commissioner in London, urging Australia to sign the constitution of the IRO, with the implication that Australia would help in resettlement of DPs.[31] Nothing happened. In May Addison wrote more urgently to Chifley:

> If it [the IRO constitution] cannot be brought into force within next two or three weeks, it looks as though the whole scheme for an international solution of refugee problem on which we have been working so hard for past eighteen months, might have to be abandoned with most disastrous consequences, not only from social and economical, but even from the political point of view. Indeed, if no solution of refugee problem is found, these unhappy people will constitute a disturbing element which may well prejudice and delay economic, social and political recovery of Europe and constitute a further element of potential friction in a situation which is already quite dangerous enough.[32]

If Calwell believed that the Pope was God's representative on earth, the more usual Australian view was that the mandate of heaven rested with His Majesty's Government in Whitehall. Australia signed as requested within a fortnight.

In June-September 1947, Calwell undertook a gruelling trip to Europe and the USA, visiting 23 countries in a last-ditch effort to find immigrants and clear the bottlenecks preventing them coming. He met mostly disappointments. Addison gave him a cordial hearing, but hinted that Britain itself faced labour shortages, and while they would not object to anyone leaving, attempts to poach workers with particular skills would not be viewed favourably. Shipping remained extremely tight (and air travel still prohibitively expensive for large numbers). A visit to Scandinavia found no potential migrants there. Discussions with the French showed them willing to spare at most a few "intellectuals such as literary workers", which was not quite what was wanted.[33] Arriving in New York, Calwell told reporters that Australia wanted at least a million Americans, a figure in line with American modes of communication but bearing no relation to reality.

The Displaced Persons proved the one bright spot. On 21 July Calwell signed an agreement with the IRO, initially for 12,000 DPs but with bigger plans in mind. Australia would select the DPs in the camps and provide work for them on arrival in Australia, with the same labour conditions as Australians. Crucially, the IRO would provide transport and pay for it (except for an extra payment per head "towards the extra costs incurred in moving immigrants to Australian ports as compared with the cost of moving them to South American ports", an indication of Australian appreciation of the problems posed by the long distances).[34]

The problems were not quite over. The two ships provided by the IRO both proved to be unseaworthy. Calwell cabled Evatt, in New York for the foundation of the United Nations, to ask if help could be found from the Truman administration. The result was the offer of an old army transport ship, the *General Stuart Heintzelman*, which was to be the first of a number of such ships which solved the shipping problem. Though substandard for migrant shipping, they were sufficient for refugees.

A small team of Australian security and medical personnel was rushed to the camps in Germany to do their best with selecting very fast a group of immigrants who would make a good impression in Australia. With an immense feat of organisation, about 850 young and healthy Baltic DPs left Bremerhaven on the *General Stuart Heintzelman* on October 30 and arrived in Fremantle on 28 November. There they transferred to *HMAS Kanimbla* for the voyage to Melbourne, where they were greeted by Calwell on 7 December before being sent to Bonegilla, a former army camp near Albury.[35] That was the only voyage of DPs in 1947, but the program was under way.

5

Minister for Immigration: The Success of the Program (1948-49)

The first Baltic immigrants were a great success.[36] They danced fetchingly in national costume for the movie cameras and expressed in excellent though accented English their gratitude for being allowed in such a wonderful country as Australia. The selling operation went smoothly. The *Sydney Morning Herald*'s "Young migrants from Baltic revel in Australian outdoors ... first camp wedding ... all fine swimmers"[37] was surpassed by the *Catholic Weekly*'s editorial on the "amazing similarity" between the Balts and the Irish (referring not so much to racial characteristics as to their flight to the ends of the earth from the heel of a foreign oppressor).[38] Only the Communist paper, *Tribune*, seriously campaigned against the program, railing against "Calwell's Balt Fascists".[39] To be on the safe side, stories about "disturbances" and complaints by migrants were suppressed and reporters from papers that ran stories of trouble on the voyage were banned from IRO ships. The terms "Balts", "Displaced Persons" and "DPs" were retired from official communications and "New Australians" substituted.

Calwell also worked hard with the leaders of groups likely to have misgivings about the program. The RSL had doubts about migrants who might have fought on the wrong side in the War, but was also strongly anti-communist. Calwell persuaded the ACTU executive to support the program and keep a lid on rank and file discontent. As Menzies said later, the immigration program "could have been taken successfully only by a Minister who was known as a life-time Labour man of the strictest orthodoxy, and was both well-known and extremely popular at the centres of unionism."[40]

Once initial reaction proved favourable, the selection criteria were quickly extended without fanfare to include Ukrainians, old people, and almost anyone without TB.

There was still the problem of how the Australian people would react when the migrants poured off the wharves. What about the culture shock when the non-English-speaking newcomers started walking the streets, competing with Australians for jobs and housing, and causing resentment by forming ghettos, doubtless in Labor electorates? The problem was worse for Australia than for any other major recipient country, since the migrants had no local communities of their own nationalities to ease the transition. Calwell's plan was also different from that of any other major recipient country. The migrants were bonded to work as the Government directed for two years, and were housed in camps, mostly disused army camps. The official purpose was to "afford the persons concerned an opportunity to establish themselves during their period of assimilation and to avoid any competition between them and Australians for houses."[41] That gave two years' grace to make progress with the housing crisis (which the migrants could help with by being assigned to the building industry); it gave time for good news stories about the wonderful contributions of New Australians to the Snowy Mountains Scheme; and it gave time for the migrants to learn English, earn some money and begin to assimilate. In any case, it postponed most of the problem until after the 1949 election.

There was one major decision still to come which would determine the size of Australia's refugee intake. The shipping problem that was still the main bottleneck at the time of Calwell's visit to Europe was partially solved by President Truman's lending dozens of army transport ships for IRO's exclusive use. But even after the successful arrival of the first boatload, the shipping shortage remained severe. By April 1948, there had only been half a dozen voyages, amounting to a few thousand migrants. Then the program was threatened with ending before it had made any substantial impact. Faced with the deteriorating political situation in Europe that eventually led to the Berlin blockade and airlift, the US Army feared that it might have to suddenly evacuate its troops or at least their dependants from Europe. It issued a secret instruction preventing its transport ships leaving the North Atlantic and American waters.[42] Despite repeated representations from Australia, the decision was not reversed. At almost the same time, the US Congress reversed its anti-immigration policy and allowed 200,000 refugees to settle. Australia, already an unfavoured destination by the IRO because of the long turnaround time for the voyages, looked like being frozen out of the scheme altogether. Australia was only a small player, with an intake of 20,000 agreed to, and all the ships being used were suddenly unavailable.

Calwell's reaction was characteristic. If Australia was at a disadvantage by being a small player, it would become a big one. Encouraged by continuing favourable press reaction at home, Calwell added a zero to the proposed intake. On

2 July, Chifley, at Calwell's urging, cabled Truman that Australia was prepared to match the American number, if Truman would help find ships.[43] Whether Calwell actually expected to get 200,000 immigrants at this stage is not clear, but by claiming to want that number, Australia became a partner in the scheme of equal weight, in principle, to the US. As such, it could claim rights to IRO shipping that was now becoming available as the Berlin crisis blew over. Truman promised to help divert such ships to the Australian run, and the problem was solved. The new number was announced without major protests ensuing and all went smoothly from then on.

What actually arrived is shown in the following table:[44]

Poles	60,300	90% Catholic
Yugoslavs	23,300	64% Catholic
Ukrainians	19,600	57% Catholic
Latvians	19,600	12% Catholic
Hungarians	13,300	74% Catholic
Lithuanians	10,100	74% Catholic
Czechoslovakians	9,900	80% Catholic
Estonians	6,000	2% Catholic
Russians	4,900	15% Catholic
Romanians	2,200	42% Catholic
Others	12,900	
Total	182,200	

The religious affiliations were not published at the time but became clear in the 1954 Census. Another matter involving religious affiliation, pointed out by extreme Protestants suspicious of Calwell's motives, was that the figure for "British" immigrants included Maltese.

The immigrants' life in camps such as Bonegilla near Albury was from an Australian perspective harsh, but less so from the point of view of people coming from several years of near-starvation in the camps of Germany.[45] The amount of meat and butter was a surprise, and work and eventually accommodation in the community was found for most.

Behind the feel-good headlines was a certain amount of culture shock. Australian English, Australian attitudes and Australian food were strange to the new arrivals. One newly-arrived immigrant was surprised to find that the unions had declared coal black.[46] The strangeness went two ways, and Australians showed little interest in the backstories of the migrants. Some immigrants faced industrial accidents, isolation from speakers of their own language and loneliness due to the imbalance of the sexes. People whose education and professional skills might have benefited Australia were stuck in assembly-line jobs. Nevertheless, overall the story was a successful one as advertised, particularly for the next generation that grew up in Australia, and Australian culture broadened artistically and intellectually.

One disappointment for Calwell and the Labor Party who had brought the DPs to Australia was that they failed to vote Labor as they chose the most anti-Communist party. Many regarded even Menzies as soft on Communism and consistently voted Democratic Labor Party (DLP) when that option became available from 1955.[47]

6

Defence of the White Australia Policy

The White Australia Policy and Calwell's especially strong defence of it are not justifiable. Nevertheless the reasons for the policy and for Calwell's views are complex, and to understand him and the Australia of his time, it is necessary to make an effort to grasp the nature of the factors involved.

The White Australia Policy excluded almost all non-whites from immigrating to Australia. It was a central reason for federation in 1901 and one of the federal parliament's first acts of legislation. The main reasons for it were twofold – fear on the part of workers of cheap foreign labour such as "Chinese coolies", and a pride in the "white race" based on an assumption that the world population was naturally divided into races with different characteristics. As with the still acceptable pride in one's country, or "black pride" or talk of "a proud Wiradjuri man", pride in belonging to a race did not necessarily imply a perception of other races as inferior, though it could easily lead to that. Calwell himself never said or did anything that implied he believed other races were inferior, even if some of his language was reasonably regarded as offensive to other races.

When Calwell came to explain his defence of the policy, as in his 1949 pamphlet 'I stand by White Australia – Appeasement never pays', one reason loomed large, and it is reasonable to infer that it really was his main reason. "Underlying the White Australia policy is no suggestion of racial superiority," he said. The problem is that mixing of races produces interracial violence, as seen in overseas countries, "the evils that plague America, that distress South Africa, that embitter Malaya, and that worry Fiji ... the evils of miscegenation always result in rioting and bloodshed." In the context of the 1940s, with apartheid rapidly developing in South Africa and the United States still in the grip of severe racial discrimination, and with few role models available of successful multiracial societies, a desire to keep Australia free of racial tensions is understandable. His views were not based on any pseudoscientific theories about race, but on the observed troubles of multiracial societies.[48]

Calwell did not however comment on whether he believed that aboriginal Australians could be part of a successful multiracial society. (He later wrote "If any people are homeless in Australia today, it is the Aboriginals. They are the only non-European descended people to whom we owe any debt. Some day, I hope, we will do justice to them."[49])

Having decided on a strong commitment to White Australia, it was then necessary to decide how strictly to maintain it. The policy had never been watertight – although many Chinese and Pacific Islander workers were deported after 1900, communities of those who were more firmly settled continued to exist with the full rights of Australian citizens. A Chinese restaurant or a trader could bring in family members to work and their children born locally were Australians. Maoris were allowed. Broome remained a multiracial town. In an embarrassing incident at the time of Indian independence in 1947, a ship arrived in Western Australia with hundreds of Anglo-Indians and it was discovered that "Anglo-Indian" meant persons of mixed race; they were quietly let in, the matter hushed up, and those responsible told not to do it again.[50]

The word "appeasement" in the title of Calwell's pamphlet refers to a problem that inevitably follows from policing a boundary – if the policing is not strict, the boundary just moves somewhere else and the problem recurs. As he put it, "How can you administer a rigid law flexibly? Either you stand by the law or you do not. Either you believe in the maintenance of a White Australia or you water down the policy."[51]

But at the end of the Second World War, a special problem arose from several thousand refugees from the Dutch East Indies and nearby who had been given temporary asylum during the War and were now expected to go home. Most did so but several hundred wished to stay, including some who had married Australians. A few Australian troops with the occupation forces in Japan wished to bring home Japanese brides. Would there be a crack in the barrier of White Australia to allow those humanitarian cases to stay?

Calwell's answer was a firm no, and a great deal of high-profile theatre ensued.

The most prominent case, which occupied news

headlines in early 1949, was that of Mrs O'Keefe. Annie Maas Jacob, a native of the eastern (later) Indonesian islands, and her family were evacuated to Australia in 1942. Her husband died in a plane crash on active service and she subsequently married her landlord John O'Keefe, a retiree. In January 1949 she and her eight children were issued with a deportation order. Her case attracted widespread sympathy in the press and many appeals were made, including one from Archbishop Mannix. Unfavourable publicity followed in South-East Asia.

Calwell replied in parliament,

> We can have a white Australia, we can have a black Australia, but a mongrel Australia is impossible, and I shall not take the first steps to establish the precedents which will allow the flood gates to be opened. I respect Asiatic people. I do not regard them as inferiors, but they have a different culture and history, different living standards and different religions from our own. They can live, and, I hope, enjoy whatever they can get from the earth's bounty in their own countries. We can make a success of our democracy here.[52]

Money was raised by Mrs O'Keefe's supporters for an appeal to the High Court. The Court upheld her appeal on the technical ground that she had not been properly designated as a prohibited immigrant on arrival. It was the first court defeat for the White Australia policy.[53]

Calwell responded by having passed a Wartime Refugees Removal Act, but before much action could be taken on the basis of it, the Labor government lost office in the 1949 election. The new Minister for Immigration, Harold Holt, permitted the remaining Asian war evacuees to stay.

Although Calwell was undoubtedly sincere in policing the boundaries in cases like that of Mrs O'Keefe, the publicity surrounding them also acted as a smokescreen for the Displaced Persons policy. While newspaper attention was focussed on Calwell's zeal in keeping out a tiny number of Asians, the floodgates were admitting 170,000 Eastern Europeans with, to a degree, "different culture and history, different living standards and different religions" from the majority of Australians.

Calwell was unfairly accused of racism over his 1947 joke that "Two Wongs do not make a White." He was answering a question from the Liberal member for Balaclava, Thomas White, about a Mr Wong who had received a deportation order. Calwell concluded his answer with "There are many Wongs in the Chinese community, but I have to say – and I am sure that the honourable member for Balaclava will not mind me doing so – that two Wongs do not make a White." The play on White's name obviously involved no racism, and the subsequent beat-up implying that Calwell had said that two Chinese are not worth one white man confirmed everything Calwell said about the irresponsibility of the press.[54]

Calwell maintained good personal relations with the local Chinese community and intervened positively in immigration cases where it could be done without publicity. He learned to speak some Mandarin.[55]

In later life, Calwell's championing of the White Australia policy was increasingly out of alignment with public opinion. In the mid 1960s, it was one of the causes of his deputy, Gough Whitlam's, frustration with his leadership. He did his reputation no favours in 1972, almost at the end of his life, by criticising coloured immigrants who "live on the smell of an oily rag and breed like flies".[56]

7

Two faiths: Socialism and Catholicism

Calwell's fight was not just with the press, but with the entire system of "monopoly capitalism", whose tool he thought the press was. Like many Labor men who had grown up in harsh circumstances, such as Scullin and Chifley, he maintained an undying enmity to the capitalists who he believed were responsible for the ills of the workers. He expressed those views in Parliament more often and forcefully than most. In a 1941 speech, he said:

> The capitalist system which honorable members opposite are trying to bolster up was responsible for all the misery and degradation incidental to the Depression period, and unless it be ended it will bring about more suffering and more poverty after this war. The Labor Party does not exist to mend the capitalist system, but to end it. If the Labor Party does not end it, that system will eventually destroy the Labor Party as we know it.
>
> Larry Anthony (Country Party) interjecting: What do the people do with all these profits?
>
> Calwell: They pay them into the funds of the United Australia Party and the United Country Party in order that their nominees may be elected to the National Parliament and do their bidding. The interjection of the honorable member is typical of that bovine mentality which this

> Parliament has long since learned to associate with membership of the Country Party.[57]

While the reply to the interjection works well as a joke, it does also suggest that Calwell had little understanding of real capitalists. He did not consort with captains of industry, nor does he appear to have grasped their claims that their entrepreneurship and innovation were essential to creating wealth that could potentially be shared.

Speaking on the *Communist Party Dissolution Bill* in 1950, Calwell ignored repeated orders by the Speaker to keep to the topic, so as to pursue his argument that Communism would never be stopped unless capitalism was. He said

> The Government claims, very piously, that it wishes to protect the community and the nation. The fact is that under our democratic system the community and the nation can protect themselves very well not only from communism and fascism but also from the ruthless and hungry monopoly of capitalism which these self-appointed protectors propose to reimpose on them. What the reactionary forces in this country really want, and what they ask for, is the right to establish and maintain a regime of poverty, insecurity, inequality, depression and malnutrition if they can do so. The system that they represent, to me and to every other true Labor man, is as bad as Communism itself. Like Communism it is a system that can be maintained only by force and fraud ... Communism is a danger throughout the world and it was created by the forces of capitalism.

> Do honorable members really want to get rid of communism? If they do, they should first get rid of capitalism.[58]

Calwell was therefore one of the most enthusiastic supporters of Chifley's 1947 announcement that banks would be nationalised. It proved to be the government's most unpopular move and a major factor in the defeat of 1949. As the rising tide of prosperity in the 1950s and 1960s made voters more relaxed with the existing economic order, old slogans about the evils of capitalism came to seem antiquated and Labor had to adjust. During the election campaign of 1961, his first as leader, Calwell said:

> despite all that has been said and will be said to the contrary, Labor has no plans to nationalise the banks or to socialise medicine or to do anything other than what is stated in this policy speech. For one thing, we have no power to nationalise without first referring the matter to you by way of referendum. We promise not to raise the question of nationalisation during the lifetime of the twenty-fourth Parliament.[59]

His meaning is clear: he would like to pursue socialist policies but the mood of the electorate will not allow him. It is no way to look like a man of the future. As with his support of the White Australia policy, Calwell's ideas were coming to be seen as of the past.

Calwell's other faith was Catholicism. Most Australian prime ministers have been Christian, but in a low-key and non-denominational style.[60] Calwell believed the full Catholic faith literally – that Jesus was God, that he founded the institutional Catholic Church to continue his work, and that everyone is called on by God to commit to objective ethics and make the world a better place. He wrote "I wish to emphasize that in all doctrinal matters I have given unquestioning obedience to what I was taught to believe, first by my dear mother and secondly through my reading and my participation in the life of the church."[61] It has to be wondered whether his very public commitment to orthodox Catholicism was an obstacle to his ambition to be prime minister. It is true that in Labor circles Catholic attendance at mass could be a positive for networking, as the same people took up the plate at mass, voted at Labor branches and attended the communion breakfasts of Catholics in unions.[62] But in the sectarian atmosphere that continued in Australian life up to the 1960s, Catholicism could also attract suspicions, from both Protestants and the far left. Many on the left remembered his involvement with anti-Communist Catholic Action in the 1940s.

Calwell's personal relationship with Mannix was also a significant part of how he thought about his faith. B.A. Santamaria said that Calwell "idolised" Mannix, and the word is not too strong.

The deep importance to Calwell of his Church in general and Archbishop Mannix in particular was the source of his entirely gratuitous and pointless attack in 1945 on the Vatican's choice of an Australian cardinal. The office is the highest one in the church other than pope, and Australia had had only one holder before, the Irish-born Cardinal Moran in the late nineteenth century.

Appointment of another one was expected, and the choices were the aged, distinguished and intelligent Irish-born Archbishop Mannix of Melbourne, or the young, not especially distinguished but Australian-born Archbishop Gilroy in Sydney. In line with general Church policy, the papal representative in Australia, Apostolic Delegate Archbishop Panico, was charged with promoting native-born clergy to positions of influence. Behind the scenes, another factor was Mannix's defiance in earlier decades of Vatican instructions to avoid public involvement in Irish republican politics – as Mannix himself said, "If I had ever wanted to be a Cardinal, I would certainly have charted my life differently."[63]

At Christmas 1945, the choice of Gilroy was announced. Most Australian Catholics welcomed the honour to their Church. Calwell was enraged that Mannix had been overlooked. It was quite inappropriate diplomatically for a Minister of the Crown to object to a Vatican decision, nor was it normal for a Catholic layman to challenge ecclesiastical appointments. Calwell was undeterred. According to his own later account of the matter:

> On December 24, 1945, I became the first Catholic layman in the English-speaking world to challenge a Papal appointment. My action brought me a lot of trouble. It happened when I heard on the radio of the appointment of Archbishop Norman Gilroy, of Sydney, to the College of Cardinals. Having gone home at lunch time, I prepared a statement and issued it to the

press.

The statement was made at a time when I was Minister for Information and Immigration in the Chifley Government. Emphasizing that I was speaking as a Catholic layman only, I said:

> The news that Archbishop Gilroy has been created a Cardinal will be received with very mixed feelings by Australian Catholics. While there will be congratulations for the new Cardinal, widespread consternation and bitter resentment will be felt that the honour which rightly belongs to the Archbishop of Melbourne, Dr Mannix, should have gone elsewhere, and to quite a comparatively junior member of the Australian hierarchy.
>
> It has been the hope of Australian Catholics in the past twenty-five years that when the Vatican decided to confer this very long overdue distinction on Australia, it would select for the honour its greatest ecclesiast, the Archbishop of Melbourne, whose magnificent intellect has shed lustre on his church, and dominated its councils, for the thirty-three years he has been in Australia.[64]

While Calwell did not direct any personal invective at Gilroy, he did towards Panico ("whose limited ability and equally limited knowledge of Australia and

Australians has ill-fitted him to influence the destinies of the Australian church"). Calwell's style of lay Catholicism was not of the "pray, pay and obey" variety. In the 1950s, he identified with the more liberal voices in the Church who would successfully change the Church in the Second Vatican Council in the early 1960s. The issue that most interested Calwell was one on which there was to be a very significant change. Catholic political theory up to that point favoured in principle a close relation between Church and state, with the state explicitly favouring the Catholic Church. Calwell argued for the separation of Church and state found in Anglophone democracies, the position adopted by the Council.[65]

In 1964, a brown paper parcel arrived at Calwell's office. It proved to contain a document from Rome in Latin, of obscure meaning. Translated, it revealed that Calwell was now Knight Commander of the Order of St Gregory the Great with Grand Silver Star. Though it had no detailed citation, he later heard it was awarded in honour of his general devotion to the Church, the possibility (by then remote) of becoming prime minister, and his work on postwar immigration.[66] It was well deserved.

The logical compatibility or otherwise of the two faiths, socialism and Catholicism, was a personal problem for Calwell as it had been for the many Catholics who had joined and in some places dominated the Labor Party. The matter was a complex one. Some versions of socialism and Catholicism were incompatible, but certain accommodations could be made to render it possible to accept both.

In the European context of the nineteenth and twentieth centuries, the Catholic Church tended to be aligned with conservative forces, partly driven by a fear of Communism. However the oppression of workers following the Industrial Revolution posed a moral problem to which a response was needed. Beginning with Pope Leo XIII's encyclical *Rerum Novarum* of 1891, the Catholic Church developed a response of "social justice". There is probably no aspect of Catholic theory as poorly understood by Protestants and other outsiders as this teaching. Yet it is one of the most significant and unique contributions of Catholicism to modern thought.

Catholic social justice theory holds that objective ethics applies not just to personal morality but to the economic and political organisation of society. Unrestrained capitalism is unjust, and so is the extreme form of socialism that would abolish private property. Instead society should be organised as a cooperative complex of interest groups constrained by justice. A society should consist of many independent institutions of different sizes and purposes cooperating in the context of an acceptance of moral rules. Families, trade unions, guilds, businesses, churches, clubs, and the state should pursue their own aims, respecting each other's spheres of action and working together to build a just society. The plan deals with principles, not political specifics, which can be left for negotiations to work out once the extremes of socialism and capitalism have been ruled out.[67]

Only a minority of Australian Catholics, lay or clerical, have been enthusiastic about this plan of social justice. Indeed, a majority of Australian Catholics have been barely aware of its existence. But there have been certain prominent and influential exceptions. Cardinal Moran was an early enthusiast and encouraged the new Australian Labor Party on the basis of it. The best known later supporters were Archbishop Mannix and some of his closest and most politically influential associates, Scullin, Calwell and Santamaria. Calwell wrote:

> Many anti-Labor Catholics appear to me as status-seeking, half-educated, pietistically minded introverts. It might do some of them good to read the Papal encyclical *Rerum Novarum*, issued by Pope Leo XIII in 1891, which was an arraignment of capitalism while also pointing to the deficiencies of Marxism.[68]

Partly as a result of the Catholic-Labor nexus, Catholic history took a very different course in Australia from Europe. In countries like France, the Church became identified with monarchism and reaction and lost the support of the working class. As Calwell quoted Pius XI, "The great scandal of the nineteenth century was that the workers of the world were lost to Christ." In Australia the working class, or at least a large section of it, was the Church. Vatican officials thought it might be imprudent to act too forcefully against Mannix's political involvements as "Monsignor Mannix, wrongly or rightly, enjoys a great influence upon the working classes."[69] Labor Party branches and local parish organisations overlapped and many working-class Catholics saw Labor politics as the way forward for justice for workers.

However a perennial problem for Catholic supporters of Labor was whether ALP policy was in line with *Rerum Novarum*'s social justice theory. *Prima facie*, it was, since it proposed to reform the deficiencies of the existing system by means such as legislated minimum wages, social security payments, industrial safety laws and taxation, without using revolutionary means such as abolishing private property. But the Labor platform also included a "socialisation objective", of doudtful meaning, which was something of an embarrassment to the parliamentary party but periodically pushed by left-wing unions. A compromise, in place during Calwell's time, was the 1921 "Blackburn interpretation of the socialisation objective". While favouring collective ownership to prevent exploitation, it qualified that by stating that "the Party does not seek to abolish private ownership even of any of the instruments of production where such instrument is utilised by its owner in a socially useful manner and without exploitation."[70]

The problem raised its head again after Chifley's attempted nationalisation of the banks in 1947. During the 1949 election campaign, some Catholics argued that bank nationalisation was a step too far towards real socialism and warned against voting Labor. Calwell replied with a pamphlet "What the Popes have said on capitalism and the employing class, the wage system, trades unions". More than a piece of short-term polemic, it was addressed to those "who want to see our social order founded on Christian principles" and embodies Calwell's vision of how Catholic faith should inform a plan of justice for the workers. It does not contain any text by Calwell (except a short preface) but the selections made from the documents of the popes and the Australian bishops, with the choice of which sentences to print in bold, show how Calwell sees his own efforts as embodying a larger Catholic plan. It repeats the abstract ethical language of Pius XI despite the difficulty a political audience would have reading it. For example on how private ownership is in principle limited by the common good, it speaks at a high level of general principle on how far government can go:

> To define in detail these duties when the need occurs and when the natural law does not do so, is the function of the Government ... Provided that the natural and divine law be observed the public authority, in view of the common good, may specify more accurately what is licit and what is illicit for property owners in the use of their possessions ...

Many papal statements are quoted complaining that "very many employers treated their work men as mere tools without any concern for the welfare of their souls, indeed without the slightest thought of higher interests." The only solution is "The development of an economic system in which great numbers of individual men, now without a stake in the country shall again become the owners, controllers and operators of productive property be it in the form of a farm, a shop, a workshop or a factory."[71]

These thoughts did not make much impression on Catholics. Calwell later expressed his disappointment: "Unfortunately, many Catholics have either ignored, forgotten or failed to read those encyclicals. They have developed a tradition of subservience to wealthy interests and a desire to create an impression of respectability for Catholic church leaders and those associated with them".[72]

One very relevant aspect of Catholic social doctrine was not mentioned by Calwell. It might have alarmed the Australian people if it had been. The earth's resources are provided by God to be shared for all. It is unjust if they are locked up as private property by some, when others lack necessities. That applies to rich capitalists who are not paying a living wage to their workers. For the same reasons, it applies to rich countries possessing excess lands when others such as refugees are without land – Australia and the United States, for example. Urging the American bishops to campaign for higher refugee intakes at Christmas 1948, Pope Pius XII wrote "Since land everywhere offers the possibility of supporting a large number of people, the sovereignty of the State, although it must be respected, cannot be exaggerated to the point that access to this land is, for inadequate or unjustified reasons, denied to needy or decent people from other nations, provided of course, that the public wealth, considered very carefully, does not forbid this".[73] In plain terms, that means that a country such as Australia has a strict obligation to take in a reasonable quota of refugees. Calwell naturally did not put that to the Australian people. Since he believed that the immigrants would be good for Australia, he did not experience any conflict between the rights of the refugees and the good of the country.

Vatican efforts on behalf of the Displaced Persons, like other Cold War matters, were handled by the very able and energetic Undersecretary of State, Giovanni Battista Montini, later Pope Paul VI. When Mannix's coadjutor archbishop, Justin Simonds, visited Europe in 1946 to investigate on behalf of the Australian bishops, Montini provided him with a car to tour the camps and see the refugee situation first-hand; he kept Calwell informed.[74]

In 1949, when the Displaced Persons immigration scheme was well under way, Calwell received a letter from Montini. The letter concludes:

> His Holiness prays that Your Excellency's activity in the field of immigration may continue to open up new avenues of life for the many thousands of people whose future at the moment seems bereft of hope, and, as a token of his paternal benevolence, He imparts to you His Apostolic Blessing.[75]

It would be possible to regard this as no more than a piece of polite Italianate officialese. On the face of it, the language is far from effusive. That is not how Calwell read it. He wrote requesting a cleaner copy, and distributed copies to those in the Catholic Church who had most enthusiastically worked to promote immigration, including Mannix. He replied to Montini:

> I was deeply touched by the expression of the

> Supreme Pontiff's paternal regard when he bestowed His Apostolic Blessing on me and on the work in which I am engaged as Minister of State in the Commonwealth of Australia. It is most gratifying to know that the work of arranging for the settlement of an ever increasing number in Australia of Displaced Persons from European countries meets with such august approval and evokes such touching commendation ... I ask you to accept the assurance that no letter which I have written in the six years in which I have been privileged to hold Ministerial office in this country has given me greater pleasure than this acknowledgement of the Holy Father's appreciation of my humble efforts in the cause of distressed humanity.[76]

The – possibly excessive – superlatives in which he expresses his pleasure at the Pope's message are revealing of his motives. Distressed humanity, as well as the Australian people, had much to thank Calwell for.

8

Deputy Leader and the Labor Split (1950-59)

The Chifley Government fell at the election of 1949 and Robert Menzies became Prime Minister. The old era truly ended with the sudden death of Ben Chifley, still Leader of the Opposition, on 13 June 1951.

Labor was not to return to power until 1972, and was in office for only three years of the thirty from 1949. Despite high hopes for electoral success in 1954, 1961, and 1969, no breakthrough came and Menzies and his successors were able to mould Australia in their own image.

That image, it is true, owed much to the Chifley years, even if Menzies did not say so. Interventionist government continued and Labor's reforms in social security were retained and extended. In immigration, the new minister, Harold Holt, vigorously pursued similar policies to Calwell's, with large numbers of Italians and Greeks added to the mix of Europeans coming to Australia as assisted migrants. The growth and transformation of the Australian population envisaged by Calwell thus continued "under new management". Continuity was assured by retaining Heyes and Armstrong in charge of the Department of Immigration.

A considerable part of the reasons for Labor's failure to regain office lay with the Party's decision on leadership after Chifley's death. Calwell was spoken of as a possible contender, but announced he would not stand and the Deputy Leader, Dr Evatt, was elected unopposed. Calwell won the ballot for Deputy Leader and remained in that position throughout the 1950s.

Evatt's leadership proved disastrous. Yet the Party failed to end it until 1960.

Evatt had an early success as leader of the successful campaign against Menzies' 1951 referendum to ban the Communist Party. But that itself stored up trouble for the future, as it allowed Labor to be portrayed as "soft on Communism". The issue proved an Achilles heel for Labor, as a section of the left of the Party was pro-Communist, and in the decade of the Korean War and the Soviet invasion of Hungary, most of the electorate was in no mood to tolerate anything of the kind.

Rather than calming the issue, Evatt exacerbated it by his astounding behaviour over the Petrov affair and the Labor Split. Labor was on track to win the election of 1954 and in fact gained over half of the two-party preferred vote.[77] But shortly before the election Soviet agents Vladimir and Evdokia Petrov spectacularly defected, claiming (as it turned out correctly) that there was a ring of Soviet spies in Australia. It raised Cold War anxieties and favoured Menzies' electoral prospects. Embittered in defeat, Evatt believed the Petrov affair was a conspiracy by Menzies. He wrote to the Soviet Foreign Minister, Molotov, asking if there were Soviet spies in Australia, then read Molotov's denial in Parliament. Some regarded Evatt's naïve reading of Molotov's letter as the most astonishing thing ever said in the Australian Parliament. Evatt then recklessly defended two of his staff who were accused in the Royal Commission on Espionage called by Menzies. The Royal Commission withdrew his leave to appear after his unsubstantiated claims in court.

Worse came at around the same time. Evatt believed there was a right-wing conspiracy within his own party as well, and in October 1954 denounced B.A. Santamaria's shadowy "Movement" as a hostile body within the Labor Party. Santamaria's largely Catholic Movement had been working since the early 1940s to roll back Communism in unions and Labor branches, with considerable success by the early 1950s. As a result of Evatt's denunciation, the Labor Party split violently, especially in Victoria and Queensland, and the large number of supporters of Santamaria were expelled. The Split created immense bitterness on both sides and rendered Labor almost unelectable. The expellees formed a right-wing Democratic Labor Party, which achieved only minor electoral success but directed its preferences to the Liberals, helping keep them in office.

Calwell's role at the centre of these events was personally very difficult for him and not productive of any good for the Party. In the 1940s he had secretly cooperated with the forces within the Party opposing Communist infiltration, as had come to light in the extraordinary case of W.T. "Diver" Dobson. An anti-Communist activist in the Federated Clerks Union, Dobson dragged himself from Sydney Harbour on 6 August 1949 and claimed to have been thrown from a Manly ferry by Communists who had stolen his documents. This story was soon found to be false. The Communist paper *Tribune* then printed sensational claims from Dobson's diary about collaboration between right-wing unionists and the security services. These were also false.[78] One true fact was that Calwell had helped Dobson obtain an office telephone line, about which he was queried in Parliament. Calwell admitted he had been fooled by Dobson, but the significant revelation was that he had used his official position to assist anti-Communist groups in a union – though Santamaria told him he had not used it enough.[79]

By this time, however, Calwell, like many other Labor men with no sympathy for Communism, was becoming alarmed by the extent and growing power of Santamaria's organisation, based on Catholic parishes and aimed solely at breaking Communist influence in unions and the Labor Party. Santamaria himself believed that Calwell's growing antipathy also had a personal element, as the two were both proteges of Mannix and he, the younger, had effectively supplanted the older Calwell as Mannix's favourite. Santamaria recalled meeting Calwell by chance in a Melbourne bookshop not long after the death of Calwell's son. Santamaria expressed sympathy but Calwell said "I don't want sympathy from you."[80]

Nevertheless, there was no doubt about Calwell's own position on Communism. In 1949, at the time the Communist-inspired Coal Strike was sapping Labor's chances of being returned at the coming election, Calwell gave free and frank expression to his views on Communists at a public rally: "A screaming collection of pathological exhibits ... this human scum ... the only places for these people are concentration camps ... pack of dingoes ... if these people were to go to Russia, Stalin wouldn't even use them for manure."[81] And in his 1961 policy speech, he said:

> We are completely and irrevocably opposed to Communism on ideological and philosophical grounds. Communism to us is an alien creed based on tyranny and sustained by terror. We have always declared, and we say it again, that between the Labor Party and the Communist Party there exists an unbridgeable gulf and that is why we always give the Communist candidate our last preference vote.[82]

By 1954, the party badly needed a leader with better anticommunist credentials, and better mental health, than Evatt. Arguably, Calwell's duty as deputy leader was to challenge for leadership. He did so. After Evatt's speech on the Movement but before the Party had definitively split, an angry Caucus meeting on 20 October 1954 considered a motion to spill all leadership positions. Calwell had announced he would stand for leader if the motion was successful.[83] The motion was lost 52 votes to 28. There was no more success with a harebrained scheme early in 1955 to roll Evatt on the pretext that he had accidentally failed to renew his ALP membership.[84] Thereafter loyalty to Evatt was taken to be the test of loyalty to the Labor Party. Calwell was attacked both by those who had left the party to form the DLP – many of them his former allies – and by Evatt loyalists within the party.

The Catholic aspects of the Split were also very painful for Calwell. In Melbourne, the centre of the

Split, Mannix had long been closely involved with Santamaria's plans and after the Split very publicly supported him. Before the 1958 election, Mannix issued a statement that included the sentence, "Every Communist and every Communist sympathizer in Australia wants a victory for the Evatt party".[85] That was especially agonising for Calwell as a long-time admirer of Mannix, and he also became the object of vicious attacks by those Melbourne Catholics who saw his staying in the Party as a betrayal. He wrote later:

> The one time when Archbishop Mannix hurt me, and hurt me deeply, was after the 1955 Labor Party split. He addressed a conference of his clergy and laid down the guidelines for functions to which he was to be invited, whether they followed church services or not. He said the priests could invite whatever public figures they liked, but he added: 'I will not appear with any of those who have been false to their principles.' Of course, it followed naturally and inevitably that every Catholic politician, Federal or State, who refused to join the DLP was excluded from church functions. The order affected me directly and greatly.[86]

It was not literally true that he was refused communion in churches, as sometimes said, but he did find it more comfortable to move to an inner-city parish that was more tolerant of political diversity.

The Split and Evatt's instability left little energy for taking the fight up to the Menzies Government, which cruised to successive victories in 1955 and 1958. The ALP did not choose to change leaders either time.

Finally, another harebrained scheme to get rid of Evatt was thought up. Despite his obviously failing mental health, the New South Wales Labor government was leaned on to appoint him as the state's chief justice. Half of the cabinet were unhappy with the ethics, but the deal was done.[87]

9

Opposition Leader (1960-67)

Even with a new team, consisting of Calwell and his young and dynamic deputy, Gough Whitlam, the chances for Labor in the 1961 election did not seem high. After its poor result in 1958, it needed 17 seats to win. Menzies was understandably confident that "There are no circumstances which would suggest even a remote possibility of the opposition winning 17 seats." But a minor venture by the government into what was later called deregulation, the scrapping of import controls, had resulted in a rush of imports that caused a balance of payments crisis and serious inflation. The government had reacted with a deflationary "credit squeeze". Businesses had contracted and unemployment doubled to a then-unacceptable 3.5%. Labor promised better social services and import controls.[88]

Calwell received an unexpected approach from R.A.G. Henderson, his foe in the censorship crisis of 1944, who, at the behest of proprietor Warwick Fairfax, offered the editorial support of the usually conservative *Sydney Morning Herald* and journalistic help in writing Calwell's speeches. The paper had never supported Labor and it was regarded as such a reversal of the natural order of things that some journalists believed the grossly unlikely rumour that Menzies had years earlier had an affair with Fairfax's first wife. Fairfax was cut at his club and Henderson's granddaughter was ostracised by some pupils at her North Shore school.[89] Support also came from the unusual quarter of capitalist manufacturers, who preferred the protectionist policies that were generously supporting key industries.

On polling day, December 9, an unexpected swing, especially in Queensland, gained Labor 15 seats and an estimated 50.5% of the two-party-preferred vote. Counting in the last seats dragged on. Eventually Menzies gained a two-seat majority with the victory in Moreton of Jim Killen, whose majority of 130 votes included not only many DLP preferences but 93 from the Communist Party candidate.[90] Labor actually won 62 seats, the same as the Coalition, but two of those seats were in the Australian Capital Territory and Northern Territory, which did not then count for purposes of forming a government. It was the closest of close shaves for Menzies, and for Labor an understandable feeling of having been robbed.[91]

Some Labor men muttered darkly that the loss despite a majority of votes was due to an error made in the massive electoral redistribution of 1948, in which powerful Labor members were said to have shored up their majorities at the expense of leaving marginal electorates unwinnable. Calwell, it was noted, was the minister most responsible as Minister for Information – indeed, his large expansion of Parliament was an achievement he was proud of.[92] However a detailed analysis shows that the Electoral Commissioners behaved fairly and that it was inevitable that Labor votes were wasted in huge majorities in inner-city seats like Calwell's Melbourne.[93]

After the near-win in 1961, Labor had considerable

hopes for the election of 1963, although they had no particular new policy that appealed to voters. The general good health of the economy, unlike in 1961, favoured the government.

The men who ruled Labor shot themselves in the foot. In March 1963, the policy-determining body of the ALP, the federal conference, met at the Kingston Hotel, Canberra. It consisted of six delegates from each state. The main issue of contention was a proposed US communications base on North West Cape, Western Australia, which would communicate with nuclear submarines and hence tie Australia militarily more closely to the US. The Labor left opposed this extension of "US imperialism", the right backed it. A vote against would tag Labor again as "soft on Communism". As midnight on 20th March approached, the votes were evenly balanced. The action was observed from outside by a leading member of the Canberra press gallery, Alan Reid. He had earlier been an ALP member and Calwell had tried to have him expelled from the Party. He now represented the *Daily Telegraph*, part of the empire of pro-Menzies press baron Frank Packer, and was on the lookout for one of the "Labor Split Looms" stories that the Packer press could usually be relied on to run before an election. What he saw, as midnight passed, was something much more newsworthy. Calwell and his deputy, Whitlam, who were not members of the conference, were outside cooling their heels while awaiting the conference's decision. Although all press photographers had gone home, Reid saw a friend who was a scientific photographer at ANU. At Reid's request, he went home, got a camera, and returned to photograph the scene. In the early hours, one delegate changed his vote and the base was accepted as Labor policy, but the damage had been done. The *Telegraph*'s story carrying the photos ran with Reid's inspired headline that Labor's elected leaders were at the beck and call of the "36 virtually unknown men" – soon dubbed "36 Faceless Men" – who really ran the Labor Party. The combination of photos and slogan made it one of the most memorable and effective of all Australian political stories.[94]

The American base was not the only issue on which the faceless men hobbled the Labor Party platform and contributed to Labor's defeat. State aid for church schools had been the main political aim of Catholics since its withdrawal around 1880. Catholics resented that they had to pay taxes for state schools and then pay again for their own schools, despite their being mostly the poorer classes of the community. Although Catholics were strong in the Labor Party, they hoped in vain for action from them. The Federal Executive resolutely opposed state aid, not only for anti-religious reasons but because they feared a sectarian backlash if the Party was seen to favour Catholics. Menzies, a self-described "simple Presbyterian" who had expressed support for state aid as far back as 1943, saw his opportunity. He promised funding for science blocks, an expensive new item that the cash-strapped Catholic schools could ill afford. The promise won votes and was a factor in the long process of Catholic voters moving away from their traditional support for Labor.

A short book written by Calwell with the help of his

talented press secretary, Graham Freudenberg, *Labor's Role in Modern Society*, detailed Labor's past glories but did not create much inspiration for the future.

President Kennedy's assassination the week before the election may or may not have had some effect. Labor lost ten seats to the Coalition.

The major issue of the federal election of 1966, Calwell's last as leader, was the Australian commitment of troops to the Vietnam War. The issue was a deeply divisive one. Public opinion in 1966 favoured the commitment, to Labor's disadvantage.

While the Australian Communist Party declined in the 1950s and Communism ceased to be an internal threat, South-East Asia, Australia's region of the world, remained volatile and poor. While Mao's killings on the scale of tens of millions took place largely out of the world's sight, Communist insurgencies in closer countries had mixed fortunes. Australia had given minor assistance to the successful British counterattack in Malaya, while the large Indonesian Communist Party was largely massacred by government forces in 1965. South Vietnam became the front line during the early 1960s, as the United States committed more and more forces to counter the North-Vietnam assisted Vietcong. As of 1966, the intervention appeared to be having some success, and nothing about the future was predictable – neither the quagmire that saw Western defeat after massive death tolls (well over a million Vietnamese, 50,000 Americans, 521 Australians), nor the killings and persecutions after Communist victory, the refugees from which were to transform the Australian population from 1979 as much as those of 1949. In 1966, success in the war seemed likely enough and Australia reaffirmed its commitment to the US alliance on which its survival was presumed to depend. President Johnson's visit the month before the election was a popular success and Harold Holt's sycophantic slogan, "All the way with LBJ", caught the majority mood.

Somewhat less popular, but still with majority support initially, was conscription, which was introduced from 1964 to bolster Army numbers. Calwell remained as resolutely anti-conscriptionist as he had been in 1916 and 1942.

The Labor Party and Calwell had few answers to the tide of opinion in favour of the Holt Government. Some on the left of the party favoured Vietcong victory or believed fears of communism were greatly exaggerated, and there was considerable feeling against the US alliance. More moderate Labor opinion was caught between opposing extremes.

Calwell's 1965 speech opposing Menzies' Vietnam commitment – largely written by Freudenberg – has become something of a classic among Australian political speeches for its defence of moral principle in the face of likely political defeat. Calwell said:

> We do not think it is a wise decision. We do not think it is a timely decision. We do not think it is a right decision. We do not think it will help the fight against Communism. On the contrary, we believe it will harm that fight in the long term. We do not believe it will promote the welfare of the

> people of Vietnam. On the contrary, we believe it will prolong and deepen the suffering of that unhappy people so that Australia's very name may become a term of reproach among them. We do not believe that it represents a wise or even intelligent response to the challenge of Chinese power. On the contrary, we believe it mistakes entirely the nature of that power, and that it materially assists China in her subversive aims ... our present policy will, if not changed, surely and inexorably lead to American humiliation in Asia ... Preoccupied with the idea of monolithic, imperialistic Communism, we have channelled our support to those military regimes which were loudest in their professions of anti-Communism, no matter how reactionary, unpopular or corrupt they may have been.

Then he admits that his position is not going to win votes:

> And may I, through you, Mr. Speaker, address this message to the members of my own Party – my colleagues here in this Parliament, and that vast band of Labour men and women outside: The course we have agreed to take today is fraught with difficulty. I cannot promise you that easy popularity can be bought in times like these; nor are we looking for it. We are doing our duty as we see it. When the drums beat and the trumpets sound, the voice of reason and right can be heard in the land only with difficulty. But if we are to have the courage of our convictions, then we must do our best to make that voice heard. I offer you the probability that you will be traduced,

> that your motives will be misrepresented, that your patriotism will be impugned, that your courage will be called into question. But I also offer you the sure and certain knowledge that we will be vindicated; that generations to come will record with gratitude that when a reckless government wilfully endangered the security of this nation, the voice of the Australian Labor Party was heard, strong and clear, on the side of sanity and in the cause of humanity, and in the interests of Australia's security.[95]

Calwell's own speaking voice is probably more authentically heard in his election speech which specifically attacked conscription in the case of a war where the nation's opinion was divided:

> Conscription is immoral, it is unjust and it is a violation of human rights. It must and will be defeated.
>
> There are 600,000 Australian mothers with sons between 15 and 20 years of age and many of these boys could be sent away to die or be wounded in the long, cruel dirty war that is raging in Vietnam.
>
> I call on those 600,000 mothers and their husbands and their other sons and daughters to tell Mr. Holt that the lives of their eligible sons are too precious to be squandered by the man who has pledged this country to go all the way with L.B.J.
>
> I doubt if any one of the Government's Senators and Representatives who voted for conscription, and

that includes the splinter group duo [the DLP], has a son fighting in Vietnam.

It is so easy, therefore, for all these anti-Labor Members of Parliament to regard the lives of other people's children as expendable and to dispose of them in any way they think fit and without remorse or regret.[96]

The 1966 campaign was also impacted by rising tensions between Calwell and his deputy Gough Whitlam. In addition to purely personal differences, they represented different visions of Labor, with Whitlam hoping to broaden the party's appeal to the newly tertiary-educated middle classes who saw themselves as progressive. The flashpoint issue was the old one of state aid to church schools. The Federal Executive of the party decided to keep to old policy and not to match Menzies' promises of state aid. Whitlam decided on a "crash through or crash" approach and went on television to condemn the executive as "twelve witless men". The Executive met to expel Whitlam from the party for "gross disloyalty", with Calwell's support, but at the last moment the Queensland delegates changed sides and Whitlam was saved, 7 votes to 5. Whitlam then challenged for the leadership in caucus, but the party was not quite ready for a new era. He lost decisively to Calwell, 49 votes to 25.[97] A leadership fight in the full blaze of publicity was no basis for a convincing campaign.

The ALP's problem with DLP preferences going to the Coalition remained as bad as ever. Calwell killed tentative negotiations in 1965 towards a rapprochement.[98]

At one of the anti-conscription rallies before the election campaign truly started, Calwell became the victim of what should probably count (depending on exact definitions) as Australia's first attempt to assassinate a politician. A disaffected 19-year-old named Peter Kocan decided to make a name for himself. He was working as a factory hand when he decided to acquire a gun and shoot someone important as a way out of his own faceless existence. On the morning of 21 June, he read that Calwell would be at an anti-conscription rally at Mosman Town Hall.

Concealing his gun in his coat, a .22 rifle with the butt and barrel sawn-off, he went to the rally. On departing from the hall, Calwell was sitting in the front passenger seat of his car when he saw Kocan approaching. Thinking he wanted to say hello, Calwell was still winding the window down when Kocan fired a single shot. The bullet shattered the car window, spraying Calwell with pellets and glass.

With blood streaming from his face, Calwell slumped across the lap of his driver.

"Oh, I've been shot," he said.

Calwell quickly recovered from his minor injuries. Kocan was found guilty of attempted murder and jailed, mostly in a facility for the criminally insane. Calwell visited him and in 1968 wrote to him: "If there is anything I can do to help you in future in the matter of the mitigation of your sentence ... I will do it". Kocan was released in 1976 and became a noted poet and fiction writer.[99]

Calwell was right to be pessimistic about the chances of his position winning votes. Labor went down to an historic defeat on 26 November 1966, winning only 41 House of Representatives seats to the Holt Government's 82. He attributed the loss to "the disunity in our own ranks on questions of personality and policy during the lifetime of the 25th Parliament".[100] He avoided calling a caucus meeting immediately but in the new year resigned as leader, to be succeeded by Gough Whitlam. He remained on the backbenches until the election of 1972, by which time he was the longest-serving member of parliament. Then Labor finally achieved victory after 23 years in the wilderness.

10

Later years (1967-73)

Calwell did not take a very active role in Parliament as a backbencher or in the party, and gradually weakened from the effects of osteoarthritis and diabetes. But occasionally he made an intervention. In 1967 he opposed a move by Labor senators to join with the DLP in the Senate to reject a budget proposal for increased postal charges, warning that if Labor helped to raise the pretensions of the Senate, the Senate would one day be used to destroy a Labor government.[101]

In 1967 he visited the Soviet Union, accepted a medallion with an image of Lenin, and on his return praised the Soviet Union for its modernisation. He contributed an article "A Great Russian Patriot" for a booklet, *Lenin: Through Australian Eyes* published by the Novosti Press Agency in 1970, in which he described Lenin as an "extraordinarily gifted man". The ALP, he said, was turning into "a petty bourgeois party" which would be infested by "social-climbing, status-seeking, lower-middle-class and white-collar people". Whitlam and the demographic supporting him were not named, but obviously referred to. Coming after the reaffirmation of Soviet realities in the 1968 invasion of Czechoslovakia, it was an extraordinary shift leftwards by someone who had been so fiercely anti-Communist in the past.[102]

In Parliament in 1972, Calwell claimed that during the War he had at Mannix's request approved exemption from war service for Santamaria and two other Catholic Action leaders. Now, he said, he regretted that he had helped them "dodge" military service, especially in view of later events: "I hate the fact that these people who benefited from an act of generosity on the part of the Curtin Labor Government lived to become vicious opponents of the Labor Party in the Vietnam War and supported the conscription of Australians to fight in that filthy, immoral, indefensible, genocidal civil war."[103] Santamaria denied he had ever applied for exemption from military service and threatened to sue Calwell if he repeated the claims outside Parliament. He agreed he had had an exemption, but said it was initiated by the Victorian branch of the Department of Labour and National Service. Records of wartime exemptions had been destroyed, but a document shortly came to light showing that Scullin had applied for a temporary exemption for Santamaria. In the 1990s, further documents were found in Catholic sources that confirmed Calwell's claims. Mannix had several times intervened to gain an exemption for Santamaria and Calwell had helped.[104] It was not clear if Santamaria had known about it.

It is hard to see the incident as any more than a storm in a teacup caused by Calwell's pursuit of a personal vendetta. Anti-communist organising was needed in 1942 – only a year before, prior to the German invasion of the Soviet Union, Australian Communists had impeded the war effort, while the need for anti-Communist activity after the War was predictable, as many expected a war against the Soviet dictatorship once the Nazi one had been defeated. A callup for Santamaria and the others would have seriously disrupted the organisation so there was a good case for exemption.

The same speech contains a sentence that can be left as Calwell's last word on his own story: "I have made a lot of mistakes in my life and I have gone on record as saying that half the problems that I have encountered in life I have created for myself." (But, he says, no more than half.)

In 1972, not long before he died, he published his autobiography, *Be Just and Fear Not*. It is described by Graham Freudenberg as "a moving, often bitter, account of his turbulent relationship with the two institutions he most loved, his party and his Church".[105] It does attempt to be fair to most of his opponents, but the element of payback is strong, especially when it comes to the Santamaria-aligned Catholics who denied him the prize of the prime ministership. He writes

> I am afraid that an inordinately large number of my fellow Catholics are fear-stricken, communist-hating, money-making, social-climbing, status-seeking, brainwashed, ghetto-minded people to whom the Pope is too venturesome, and not sufficiently prudent in his dealings with the non-Catholic world on the one hand and the communist one-sixth of the world on the other ... tough language, but still no tougher than the times and circumstances demand. After all, Christ did drive the money-changers out of the temple. But a majority of present day Christians of all denominations love to make friends of the mammon of iniquity... Until the Catholic church authorities

repudiate the manifestations of McCarthyism in the Catholic community and disown the activities of all those who spread their lying, vicious and unscrupulous propaganda against the Labor Party, the church generally will continue to suffer.[106]

However, on his death the DLP Senator Frank McManus said, "I am glad to say that a month before he died we met, we had a discussion and, when we parted, he wished me well and I wished him well. I do not believe that in any way he was compromising the political stance that he had taken. I understood that, as a deeply religious man, he wanted to leave this world with malice towards none. I am sure that God has been good to him. May his soul rest in peace."[107]

His wife Elizabeth died in 1981. His daughter Mary Elizabeth continued to live in the family home for decades and wrote about her father's life, notably in the 2013 book, *I Am Bound To Be True: The life and legacy of Arthur A. Calwell.*

Epilogue

The anticommunist Displaced Persons who had voted against Labor received their payback from Whitlam in 1974 when he gratuitously, for no political benefit and without consulting his Minister for Foreign Affairs recognised the incorporation of the Baltic states in the Soviet Union.[108] When South Vietnam fell to the invading North Vietnamese army in 1975, Whitlam refused to allow even those Vietnamese who were at grave risk for having worked for Australia to come as refugees. Clyde Cameron recalled him saying in Cabinet, "I'm not having hundreds of f*ing Vietnamese Balts coming into this country with their political and religious hatreds against us."[109]

In the late 1970s, the Vietnamese government proved itself a typical Stalinist regime. By 1979 50,000 people a month were fleeing in boats and the countries of southeast Asia were starting to tow them back out to sea. The situation of 1946 had recurred – a million refugees from communism sought resettlement and there was no appetite for forcing them back. The solution was also the same, in contrast to the gross failure of the world community to solve most refugee crises. The U.S. State Department and the United Nations High Commission for Refugees coordinated a plan, involving bribing the Vietnamese to stop sending them and distributing the refugees to developed countries willing to take them.[110] The Fraser government in Australia signed up for a few thousand, though there was little support in opinion polls. The eventual number admitted is hard to determine but possibly about 150,000 (the number of Vietnamese-born in the 1996 census). Sydney and Melbourne became Asian cities.

Calwell would not have approved of the result, the true end of White Australia. Nevertheless it was his doing. His transformation of the old British Australia into a successful multicultural and multilingual society made possible the next step of a successful multiracial society.

Select bibliography

Calwell, Arthur A. (1945), *How Many Australians Tomorrow?* Reed & Harris, Melbourne

Calwell, Arthur (1972), *Be Just and Fear Not*, Lloyd O'Neil in association with Rigby, Hawthorn Vic

Calwell, Mary Elizabeth (2007), "Influences, insights and implications," *Australasian Catholic Record* 84, 145-153

Calwell, Mary Elizabeth (2013), *I Am Bound To Be True: The life and legacy of Arthur A. Calwell*, Mosaic Press, Preston

Franklin, James (2009), "Calwell, Catholicism and the origins of multicultural Australia," Proceedings of the Australian Catholic Historical Society Conference, repr. in J. Franklin, *Catholic Thought and Catholic Action: Scenes from Australian Catholic Life*, Connor Court, Brisbane, 2023, ch. 12

Franklin, James, Gerald O. Nolan and Michael Gilchrist (2015), *The Real Archbishop Mannix: From the sources*, Connor Court, Ballarat, ch. 12

Freudenberg, Graham (1993), "Calwell, Arthur Augustus (1896-1973)," *Australian Dictionary of Biography*, vol. 13, Melbourne University Press, Melbourne, http://adb.anu.edu.au/biography/calwell-arthur-augustus-9667

Kiernan, Colm (1978), *Calwell: A personal and political biography*, Thomas Nelson, West Melbourne

Kunz, Egon F (1988), *Displaced Persons: Calwell's New Australians*, ANU Press, Sydney

Morgan, Patrick (2017), "The parallel careers of Arthur Calwell and Archbishop Simonds," *Journal of the Australian Catholic Historical Society* 38, 74-83

Persian, Jayne (2017), *Beautiful Balts: From Displaced Persons to New Australians*, NewSouth Publishing, Sydney

Tavan, Gwenda (2012), "Leadership: Arthur Calwell and the post-war immigration program," *Australian Journal of Politics and History* 58, 203-220

Zubrzycki, Jerzy (1995), Arthur Calwell and the Origin of Post-War Immigration, Bureau of Immigration, Multicultural and Population Research, Canberra

Calwell's papers are in the National Library of Australia.

A number of objects are displayed in the Museum of Australian Democracy's Calwell Collection, https://collection.moadoph.gov.au/collections/arthur-calwell-collection/

Endnotes

1. Colm Kiernan, *Calwell: A Personal and Political Biography*, Nelson, Melbourne, 1978, p. 119.
2. Arthur Calwell, *Be Just and Fear Not*, Lloyd O'Neil, Hawthorn, 1972, p. 103.
3. Calwell interview in Hazel de Berg collection, excerpted at https://www.portrait.gov.au/words/arthur-calwell-part-one
4. Basic biographical facts are taken from Calwell, *Be Just*; Kiernan, *Calwell* and Graham Freudenberg, "Calwell, Arthur Augustus (1896-1973)," *Australian Dictionary of Biography*, Vol. 13, Melbourne University Press, Carlton, 1993, http://adb.anu.edu.au/biography/calwell-arthur-augustus-9667
5. Mary Elizabeth Calwell, "Influences, Insights and Implications," *Australasian Catholic Record*, Vol 84, No. 2, April 2007, pp. 145-153; Calwell, *Be Just*, p. 31.
6. Kiernan, *Calwell*, p. 138.
7. Senator Thomas Drake-Brockman, obituary of Arthur Calwell, Hansard, Senate, 21 August 1973.
8. James Franklin, Gerald O. Nolan and Michael Gilchrist, *The Real Archbishop Mannix: From the Sources*, Connor Court Publishing, Ballarat, 2015, pp. 28-33.
9. *Tribune*, 8 November 1917, p. 5.
10. Calwell, *Be Just*, pp. 35-36; Kiernan, *Calwell*, pp. 27-31.
11. Sally Young, *Media Monsters: The Transformation of Australia's Media Empires*, UNSW Press, Sydney, 2023, p. 99.
12. Calwell, *Be Just*, p. 29.
13. Hansard, House of Representatives, 27 November 1940.
14. Calwell, *Be Just*, p. 53.
15. Calwell, *Be Just*, pp. 54-55.
16. Hansard, House of Representatives, 13 November 1941; Kiernan, *Calwell*, pp. 92-96.
17. Young, *Media Monsters*, pp. 106-124.
18. Young, *Media Monsters*, p. 318.
19. Kiernan, *Calwell*, pp. 68-69.

20 Quoted in Jerzy Zubrzycki, *Arthur Calwell and the Origin of Post-War Immigration*, Bureau of Immigration, Multicultural and Population Research, Commonwealth Government, Canberra, 1995, pp. 4-5.

21 Andrew Markus, "Heyes, Sir Tasman Hudson Eastwood (1896–1980)," *Australian Dictionary of Biography*, Vol 14, 1996; Calwell, *Be Just*, p. 97.

22 Barbara Mackay-Cruise, *Immigrants and Spies: My father, my memories: Noel W. Lamidey and the Birth of Australian Migration*, Xoum, Sydney, 2017.

23 Stan Arneil, *Black Jack: The Life and Times of Brigadier Sir Frederick Galleghan*, Macmillan, South Melbourne, 1983, pp. 131-45.

24 Ute von Hofmeyer, "The Employment of Scientific and Technical Enemy Aliens (ESTEA) Scheme in Australia: A Reparation for World War II?" *Prometheus*, Vol 12, 1994, pp. 77-93.

25 "Displaced Persons accepted as migrants," *Canberra Times*, 17 July 1947, p. 1.

26 Sheila Fitzpatrick, "Migration of Jewish 'Displaced Persons' from Europe to Australia after the Second World War: Revisiting the Question of Discrimination and Numbers," *Australian Journal of Politics and History*, Vol 67, Issue 2, June 2021, pp. 226-245; Calwell, *Be Just*, pp. 101-3; Kiernan, *Calwell*, pp. 123-4; Mary Elizabeth Calwell, "Arthur Calwell and Jewish Refugees," *Centre News* (Jewish Holocaust Centre Inc), Vol 28, No. 3, Dec 2006, pp. 29-30.

27 Egon F. Kunz, *The Intruders: Refugee doctors in Australia*, Australian National University Press, Canberra, 1975.

28 David Day, *Chifley*, HarperCollins, Sydney, 2001, pp. 230-232; background in Carolyn Holbrook, "The Transformation of Labor Party Immigration Policy, 1901–1945," *Journal of Australian Studies*, Vol 40, issue 4, 2016, pp. 403-417.

29 A. James Hammerton and Alistair Thomson, *Ten Pound Poms: Australia's invisible migrants*, Manchester University Press, Manchester, 2005.

30 James Franklin, "Calwell, Catholicism and the origins of multicultural Australia," Proceedings of the Australian

Catholic Historical Society Conference, 2009, repr. in James Franklin, *Catholic Thought and Catholic Action: Scenes from Australian Catholic Life*, Connor Court Publishing, Brisbane, 2023, ch. 12.

31 Australian Archives, series A698014 item S250104, last (i.e. chronologically first) document.

32 In Beasley to Chifley, 1/5/1947, repr. in W. J. Hudson & Wendy Way, (eds), *Documents on Australian Foreign Policy 1937-49*, vol. XII, Australian Government Publishing Service, Canberra, 1995, p. 484.

33 Andrew Markus, "Labour and Immigration 1946-9: the Displaced Persons Program," *Labour History*, Vol 47, 1984, pp. 73-90.

34 Agreement with the International Refugee Organisation, 21 July 1947, https://www.dfat.gov.au/about-us/publications/historical-documents/Pages/volume-12/283-agreement-with-the-international-refugee-organisation

35 Ann Smith, "The *General Heintzelman* and the *Kanimbla*," in James Jupp, ed. *The Australian People: An Encyclopedia of the Nation, Its People and Their Origins*, Cambridge University Press, Cambridge, 2001, pp. 74-75.

36 Jayne Persian, *Beautiful Balts: From Displaced Persons to New Australians*, NewSouth Publishing, Sydney, 2017.

37 "Young migrants from Baltic revel in Australian outdoors," *Sydney Morning Herald*, 17 December 1947, p. 2.

38 "For some New Australians," *Catholic Weekly*, 18 December 1947, p. 4.

39 "Half-finished homes rot – materials, labour go to Balt hostels," *Tribune*, 20 August 1949, p. 6.

40 Robert Menzies, *Afternoon Light: Some memories of men and events*, Cassell, Melbourne, 1967, p. 59.

41 T.H.E. Heyes to Commonwealth Officer, all States, 19/9/1947, in Australian Archives, Series A6980/4, Item S2550104.

42 "Shipping for displaced persons: agenda for meeting of Commonwealth Immigration Advisory Council," in Australian Archives A6980/4 item S250105.

43 Chifley to Truman, 2/7/48, and Truman to Chifley, 19/7/48,

and Calwell's public statement, 8/7/48, AA A6980/4 item S250105; "200,000 Balts if ships given," *Argus* 9 Jul 1948, p. 7.

44 Figures for total arrivals from Table 48 of Malcolm J. Proudfoot, *European Refugees, 1939-52*, Faber, London, 1957; figures for religion from Egon F. Kunz, *Displaced Persons: Calwell's New Australians* Australian National University Press, Sydney, 1988, table 4.2, 'Religion of displaced persons in Australia in conjunction with nationality', taken from Zubrzycki's 10% survey.

45 Wanda Skowronska, *To Bonegilla from Somewhere*, Connor Court Publishing, Ballarat, 2013.

46 Catherine Panich, *Sanctuary? Remembering Postwar Immigration*, Allen and Unwin, Sydney, 1988, p. 134.

47 James Jupp, "Politics, Public Policy and Multiculturalism," in Michael Clyne and James Jupp, (eds), *Multiculturalism and Integration: A Harmonious Relationship*, ANU Press, Canberra, 2011, pp. 41-52; M.G. Cleggett, Migrants in the DLP: A Study of the Involvement of a Group of Migrants in the DLP in Victoria, M.A. Thesis, Department of Sociology, La Trobe University, 1971; Jean I. Martin, *Community and Identity: Refugee Groups in Adelaide*, ANU Press, Canberra, 1972, ch. 6.

48 Arthur Calwell, *I Stand By White Australia*, Minister for Immigration and Information, Melbourne, 1949, reprinted from the *Argus*, 24 October 1949.

49 Calwell, *Be Just*, p. 116; further in Kiernan, *Calwell*, pp. 133-4.

50 Alison Blunt, "Postcolonial migrations: Anglo-Indians in 'White Australia'," *International Journal of Anglo-Indian Studies*, Vol 5, No. 1, 2000, pp. 2-15.

51 "Migrant laws not flexible," *The Age*, 20 May 1949, p. 2.

52 Hansard, House of Representatives, 9 February 1949.

53 Sean Brawley, "Finding Home in White Australia: The O'Keefe Deportation Case of 1949," *History Australia*, Vol 11, Issue 1, 2014, pp. 128-148.

54 Hansard, House of Representatives, 2 December 1947; misreported in "Malays with two wives," *Sydney Morning Herald*, 3 December 1947, p. 4.

55 Kiernan, *Calwell*, p. 135.
56 "Parties reject Calwell view," *Canberra Times*, 3 May 1972, p. 1; basic ideas reiterated in Calwell, *Be Just*, pp. 124-7.
57 Hansard, House of Representatives, 13 November 1941.
58 Hansard, House of Representatives, 11 May 1950.
59 Calwell, Election Speech, 16 November 1961, https://electionspeeches.moadoph.gov.au/speeches/1961-arthur-calwell
60 Roy Williams, *In God They Trust?: The Religious Beliefs of Australia's Prime Ministers, 1901-2013*, Bible Society, Sydney, 2013.
61 Calwell, *Be Just*, p. 135.
62 James Franklin, "Catholic Action, Sydney Style: Catholic Lay organisations from Friendly Societies to the Vice Squad," *Journal of the Royal Australian Historical Society*, Vol 108, issue 2, 2022, pp. 172-201.
63 Calwell, *Be Just*, pp. 129-130
64 Calwell, *Be Just*, p. 128.
65 A. A. Calwell, Review of L. Webb, *Church and State in Italy 1947-1957*, *Australian Quarterly*, Vol 30, No 4, Dec 1958, pp. 112-114.
66 Calwell, *Be Just*, pp. 159-162.
67 Franklin, Nolan and Gilchrist, *The Real Archbishop Mannix*, ch. 9; Race Mathews, *Of Labour and Liberty: Distributism in Victoria 1891-1966*, Monash University Press, Clayton, Vic, 2017, ch. 1; Michael Hogan, *Australian Catholics: The Social Justice Tradition*, Collins Dove, Melbourne, 1993.
68 Calwell, *Be Just*, p. 137.
69 Franklin, Nolan and Gilchrist, *The Real Archbishop Mannix*, p. 121.
70 Troy Bramston, "The Albatross of Labor's 'Socialist Objective'," *Australian Quarterly*, Vol 74, No 4, July-Aug, 2002, pp. 27-32, 40.
71 Arthur A. Calwell, What the Popes have said on capitalism and the employing class, the wage system, trades unions, pamphlet, A.A. Calwell, Canberra, 1949.
72 Calwell, *Be Just*, p. 137.
73 Pius XII to Cardinal McNicholas, 24 December 1948, in *Acta Apostolicae Sedis*, Vol 41, pp. 69-70, quoted in 'Exsul famil-

ia', *Constitutio apostolica de spirituali emigrantium cura* (30 Sept 1952), in *Acta Apostolicae Sedis*, Vol 44, 1952: 649704, at pp. 675-87; trans. in *The Church's Magna Charta for Migrants*, ed. Giulivo Tessarolo, St Charles Seminary, Staten Island, NY, 1962, pp. 23-100, at p. 51.

74 Frank Mecham, *The Church and Migrants, 1946-1987*, St Joan of Arc Press, Haberfield, 1991, ch. 1; Max Vodola, *Simonds: A Rewarding Life*, Catholic Education Office, Melbourne, 1997, pp. 47-49.

75 Montini to Calwell, 4 April 1949, in Calwell papers, National Library of Australia, Box 62.

76 Calwell to Montini, 30 June 1949.

77 Though that figure is misleading as some seats, all but one safe Coalition seats, were uncontested.

78 Phillip Deery, "Labor, communism and the cold war: The case of 'Diver' Dobson," *Australian Historical Studies*, Vol 27, 1997, pp. 66-87.

79 Santamaria to Calwell, 24 July 1944?, in Patrick Morgan, (ed), *B.A. Santamaria: Your Most Obedient Servant*, Miegunyah Press, Carlton, 2007, pp. 5-10.

80 B.A. Santamaria, interview in Film Australia's *Australian Biography* series, 1997, transcript at https://www.nfsa.gov.au/collection/curated/australian-biography-bob-santamaria

81 "What Calwell thinks of Communists," *Weekly Times* (Melbourne), 3 August 1949, p. 4.

82 Calwell, Election speech, 16 Nov 1961, https://electionspeeches.moadoph.gov.au/speeches/1961-arthur-calwell

83 "Evatt supporters confident of Caucus vote," *Barrier Daily Truth*, 19 October 1954, p. 1.

84 Jack Kane, *Exploding the Myths: The Political Memoirs of Jack Kane*, Angus & Robertson, North Ryde, 1989, pp. 68-71.

85 Franklin, Nolan and Gilchrist, *The Real Archbishop Mannix*, p. 256.

86 Calwell, *Be Just*, pp. 141-2.

87 David Clune, "Reg Downing: A Safe Pair of Hands," in Ken Turner and Michael Hogan, (eds), *The Worldly Art of Politics*, Federation Press, Sydney, 2006, pp. 228-245.

88 David Lee, "Issues that Swung Elections: The 'Credit

Squeeze' that Nearly Swept Menzies from Power in 1961," *The Conversation*, 30 April 2019, https://theconversation.com/issues-that-swung-elections-the-credit-squeeze-that-nearly-swept-menzies-from-power-in-1961-115140

89 Young, *Media Monsters*, pp. 367-371.
90 Howard Guille, "A Nation Building Election – but the Wrong Nation?", *Queensland Journal of Labour History*, no. 23, September 2016, pp. 1-4.
91 Calwell, *Be Just*, ch. 23.
92 Calwell, *Be Just*, pp. 266-7.
93 Colin A. Hughes, "The 1948 Redistribution and the Defeat of the Chifley Government," *Labour History*, No. 34 (May, 1978), pp. 74-86; Kane, *Exploding the Myths*, p. 43.
94 Ross Fitzgerald and Stephen Holt, *Alan 'The Red Fox' Reid: Pressman Par Excellence*, University of New South Wales Press, Sydney, 2010, pp. 155-159.
95 Hansard, House of Representatives, 4 May 1965; Stephen Mills, "A certain grandeur," *Inside Story*, 29 July 2017, https://insidestory.org.au/a-certain-grandeur/
96 Arthur Calwell, Election speech, 10 November 1966, https://electionspeeches.moadoph.gov.au/speeches/1966-arthur-calwell
97 Jenny Hocking, *Gough Whitlam: A Moment in History*, Miegunyah Press, Carlton, 2008, pp. 253-256; Calwell, *Be Just*, pp. 226-232.
98 Gerard Henderson, *Santamaria: A Most Unusual Man*, Miegunyah Press, Carlton, 2015, pp. 271-3.
99 Keirnan, *Calwell*, pp. 253-256; Calwell, *Be Just*, pp 5-9; Shane Maloney and Chris Grosz, "Arthur Calwell & Peter Kocan," *The Monthly*, August 2007.
100 Freudenberg, "Calwell, Arthur Augustus".
101 Freudenberg, "Calwell, Arthur Augustus".
102 Ross Fitzgerald and Stephen Holt, "Calwell revived by Soviet visit," *The Australian*, 1 September 2012.
103 Hansard, House of Representatives, 23 February 1972.
104 Henderson, *Santamaria*, pp. 150-5.
105 Freudenberg, "Calwell, Arthur Augustus".
106 Calwell, *Be Just*, p.166
107 Hansard, Senate, 21 August 1973.
108 Michael Easson, *Whitlam's Foreign Policy*, Connor Court

Publishing, Redland Bay, 2023, p. 66.
109 Clyde Cameron, *The Cameron Diaries*, Allen and Unwin, Sydney, 1990, p. 801.
110 Barry Wain, *The Refused: The Agony of the Indochinese Refugees*, Simon and Schuster, New York, 1981, ch. 11; Nancy Viviani, *The Long Journey: Vietnamese migration and settlement in Australia*, Melbourne University Press, Carlton, 1984, ch. 5.